❈ MONTY DON ❈ EXTRAORDINARY GARDENS *of the* WORLD ❈

WEIDENFELD & NICOLSON

London Borough of Barnet

Askews	Nov-2009
712.6	£30.00

PERSONAL

SPIRITUAL

NATURAL

BOTANICAL

HISTORICAL

EDIBLE

COMMUNAL

There is a lot of clipping in a Wirtz garden, but, I was firmly told, always with an electric hedge cutter if possible or by hand, never with a petrol-driven machine. These green walls make spaces of monastic quiet and calm.

THE BOON GARDEN

OOSTZAAN, AMSTERDAM, THE NETHERLANDS

The garden of the Boon family is at Oostzaan, and, although surrounded by fields, is just twenty minutes north of the centre of Amsterdam. The garden was designed by Piet Oudolf as the house was being built specifically to integrate with the building and the personal, domestic tastes of the family.

If Jacques Wirtz's garden is like a breathing studio liable to change in the course of a day, this is a finished, self-conscious piece of design.

Oudolf has created fixed volumes (like hedges or walls) and dynamic ones that grow and change, like borders. The relationship between these two creates the energy and tension of the garden.

Ouldolf believes that borders should appear as artless as a meadow and in this he is tapping into a very modern need to escape the intense depersonalisation of the city. His plants are chosen either as species or varieties that look as though they might be species. His flowering plants are chosen as much for their form as their flowers – as flowering, he explains, is always for a relatively brief period. The result is that both in appearance and concept his designs are always confidently, coolly modern.

The proportions are everywhere solid and massively bold, tethering the garden to the ground against the enormous sky, like great green moorings. It is crisp as possibly can be at the centre, radiating from the empty blackness of the pool outwards and then gradually softening: the boundary hedge is cloud pruned, rounding the edge as it fades into sky – literally against clouds. On the other side the apple trees have the same effect.

The garden is dominated by a long pool, twenty paces by five, with raised walls 18 inches wide and 18 inches high with a wooden decking walkway around it five feet wide. The water is like glistening black rubber. A pavilion sits at the end beyond it and it is flanked on either side by more massive, low hedges, this time in yew. On one of the wettest, greyest days of an exceptionally wet, grey summer the greens shine out of the gloom. Everything is simplified down to big spaces. No mess but lots of mass.

The main beds flanking the pool are planted extremely simply – and strongly – with *Deschampsia*, *Amsonia orientalis* and the red clover *Trifolium rubrum*. But the big border seperating the pool area from the little orchard contains – or so I quickly jotted down – *Rogersia*, *Anemone*, *Thalictrum*, *Sanguisata*, *Eupatorium*, *Geranium*, *Polygonatum*, *Campanula*, *Filipendulum*, *Aconitum*, *Salix*, *Phlox*, *Sedum* and the grasses *Stipa* and *Molinia*.

MIA LEHRER GARDEN

BRENTWOOD, LOS ANGELES, CALIFORNIA, USA

This is the garden of a house that has wholly reinvented itself. Having lived on the site for decades the owners of this house decided to pull it down and start again with a brand new garden to accompany it. From the outset the garden was to have equal billing with the house. From conception, the relationship between the exterior and the interior was designed to be intimate and particular. The landscape designer Mia Lehrer worked on the garden from the outset, starting before the original building was bulldozed and salvaging many of the trees that were on the site for replanting.

Ricardo Legorreta had been an associate of Luis Barragán in Mexico City and I could immediately see the connections. There were the same huge windowless planes painted brilliant colours, the same sense of mass weighted against areas of light and almost delicate colour. The planting is inextricably entwined with the building, with architecture and plants almost dancing together. It is as much a garden with a house as a house with a garden. But for that to happen you also need the complicity – and money – of a willing client together with a cultural ethos that embraces artistic adventure. In the wealthy suburbs of LA these qualities are more available than probably anywhere else on earth.

The integration of house and garden was literal. Having gathered up existing plants – including seven enormous Washingtonian palms – there was a problem of where to store them, so they were placed into their final positions before the hosue was built and construction work took place around them.

Californian gardens are designed with the sun as an essential and almost constant element and therefore the shade is often as deep and intense as the sunshine. Lehrer brilliantly uses this to create patterned shadows.

The presence of water is also a constant. Pale honey-coloured stone steps run down the slope with a raised rill in the retaining wall on one side and a terraced lawn on the other. Stone, water and grass stepping down. This is the main view and performance and the pool is the true centre of the Californian garden. It goes back to Thomas Church in the 1950s – gardens are for people – and the unspoken subtext being that gardens are for people with swimming pools too. But swimming pools are a problem for any garden designer, falling somewhere between a trampoline and a canal or formal pond. Mia's pool seems to answer all the questions, partly through the elegance of its lines but especially through the wonderful deep Prussian blue used in the tiles.

I wondered what the future of this garden might be. If and when it is sold, will new owners pull it all down and rebuild their own version of a house and home? Will there come a time when Californians wish to preserve houses and gardens as having an historic artistic value higher than the creativity and delight of the new?

CRUDEN FARM

LANGWARRIN, MELBOURNE, AUSTRALIA

This is the garden of a matriarch, still vibrantly engaged with the modern world. It reflects an independent Australian identity but is expressed in very British ways and it is a personal expression of the woman who has made it throughout a very long life. Dame Elizabeth Murdoch was born in Melbourne in 1909. In 1928 she married Keith Murdoch, founder of the Australian newspaper dynasty. He bought his wife Cruden Farm, which was then in the countryside to the east of the city but is now in the suburbs, as a wedding present and they used it as a weekend and holiday home. It was then a small cottage with a little garden around it. Since the first years of her mariage, the garden has been made and managed entirely by Dame Elizabeth. There can be few people that have gardened continuously in the same place for eighty years, let alone with such skill and passion.

There is now just one gardener, but Dame Elizabeth did most of the work here until she was in her seventies and kept working daily into her eighties. She still oversees absolutely everything in the garden from her electric buggy and takes what she calls her 'daily trundle', charging round the place.

The walled garden (*centre*), designed by Edna Walling, is a surprisingly intimate space set amongst these giant trees and sweeping expanses of grass, but the flanking borders it contains are lovely, dominated by the blue and purple flowering spires of delphiniums. The lack of size appears as a stroke of modesty rather than a design flaw.

Behind the house is the rose and vegetable garden (*below*). The roses rise out of poppies, nepeta, alstromeiras, more delphiniums and foxgloves – a soft and lovely mix of flowers that could be found in a thousand English borders, but as she takes me round it is apparent that every rose has a story and meaning to her. They are old friends.

It is a formal garden with neatly clipped hedges, but bean sticks are reused and a pig-netting frame is stretched across what looks suspiciously like an old bedstead to support sweet peas. In short it is not all just for show, but a proper working garden designed to please those that garden and live in it as well as to impress the visitor.

Cruden farm is a garden of huge mature trees and all of them, bar one, have been planted by Dame Elizabeth. But trees grow fast in the Victorian climate.

You approach the house and garden down a curving avenue of lemon-scented gums (opposite), *Corymbia citriodora*, with a mottled mauve bloom to the trunks and olive leaves rattling in the hot breeze. It is a bush plant, but here becomes a statement of Australian identity and a glorious, deliciously fragrant one.

At the back of the house there is a large lake (below), and in it a sizeable island with more trees and the parrot-like orange of kniphofias reflected in the water. It is Brownian in scale and scope, made balanced by the maturity of the trees set back from the water. Beyond the water is another wave of oaks, perhaps 30 feet tall, planted from the acorns of the great majestic specimens that dame Elizabeth also planted, 50 years earlier.

CASA BARRAGÁN

MEXICO CITY, MEXICO

The great Mexican architect built this house for himself in 1947. It is tucked away in a side street and from the outside is an unprepossessing, industrial-looking building. This was consistent with Barragán's belief that a house should be a refuge from the world and that its exterior should be plain and modest. But once inside, the first thing that strikes you is the extraordinary use of volume and colour, both of which are are the key to Barragan's work.

The house has a kind of luminous monastic richness. The furniture is simple and strong – all designed by Barragán. The walls are mostly white, but some are livid yellow or pink. The colours are immensely strong but not instantly recognisable. You find yourself mixing words in your head like paints on a palette to describe them. This is because they were mixed by Barragán himself, as were all the colours that he used in his buildings. These colours were strongly influenced by the yellowish dirt, the grassland, the sky and the cacti native to the flat landscape of the Mexican savannah.

Narrow stairs lead to a slim door onto the roof. I am hit by more brilliant, resounding colour. The roof garden is a completely empty space, yet it is filled with colour and shade from the high walls that go right round it.

Barragán was a deeply religious, spiritual man and his work reflects that side of him. This house, with its simple, cell-like bedroom and little dining room where he ate alone, culminates up here on the roof, wide open to the sky, with the enormous walls making a generous space seem even larger and yet private, enclosed. The colour is gorgeous, flamboyant, shimmering, sensuous. Yet it does not undermine or lessen the simplicity or spirituality.

Barragán believed that houses should be open but not overlooked. He took great trouble with these walls, and with the positioning of windows and doors: he would place the opening to line up with the landscape or garden – not the other way round.

It is a sublime, brilliant piece of gardening. Burle Marx said "a garden is nature organised by man for man". Barragan has used his genius to organise those most elusive aspects of all – light and space – through the medium of colour.

CASA GALVEZ

MEXICO CITY, MEXICO

Another of Barragán's creations, Casa Galvez is, again, a striking and intensely private space which revisits the artist's fascination with colour, volume, light and shade. This house and garden too were built at the end of the 1940s and are lived in by a family who have accepted the whole as a complete, untouchable work of art. And as at Casa Barragán, bold colour and detail are reflected inside and out.

The garden's levels are carefully manipulated with steps and low retaining walls. This was once a sloping site, which was altered by Barragán so that the huge planes of vertical walls are matched with horizontal planes of more sombre grass and paving.

The planting is loose and exuberant, but serves the colours and forms of the structure well. The bougainvillea is exactly the same furious colour as the walls. This could not work in cloud-covered Britain: the colours would appear hysterical and gaudy under a grey sky.

CASA CARUNCHO

MADRID, SPAIN

Fernando Caruncho is one of the few geniuses of garden and landscape design. His work combines a feeling for landscape, gardens, spirituality and philosophy that transcends the merely attractive or interesting and effortlessly becomes art. He designed both his own house and garden just outside Madrid and, although compared to some of the grand schemes of some of his clients they are modest in scale, it is all thrillingly beautiful. He trained as a philosopher and his reading of Euripides taught him that the Greeks made no difference between man and nature. A garden was a magical place to attract the Gods. So for Caruncho the core of good modern gardens is that they are places where God might be present – and the spiritual and philosophical aspects of his work are central to it.

Caruncho's own garden is restrained and pared down. His obsession with the grid appears in the mesh he uses as screens both on walls and ceilings, and in the shapes created by the architecture, but it is not as evident here as in many of his commissioned works where a grid of pools, tiny fields, courtyards or flat-topped or undulating blocks of green recur again and again like a musical motif.

The walls are painted a rich apricot inside and out, creating reflections of apricot light. Wire mesh squares the garden beyond into a leafy grid.

A patio with massive square columns and a mesh roof supporting wisteria has room for a table and passageway (below right).

A large pond (below) fills the entire space that the house wraps around on three sides – a watery courtyard. The other side of the water is a bank with a summer house on top of it facing the main building. Escallonia, clipped into flowing unbroken contours, covers the bank. Everything is very simple, very strong and the effect is incredibly subtle.

I ask Caruncho about his approach to design. "All gardening is simple," he says. "Planting should be simple. You must do what the poet Pope said – 'consult the genius of the place'. The invisible thing is always the most important part of a garden. If you use memory, communal history and your subconscious and try not to think, it will come. You have to let the hand do it alone."

JARDIN MAJORELLE

MARRAKECH, MOROCCO

Majorelle is a relict from the 1920s and 30s when the French influence was at its peak in Marrakech and wealthy, liberal French were attracted to this exotic, but accessible, colonial city. One of these visitors was Jacques Majorelle, a painter from Nancy who came to improve his health in 1917 and stayed here until his death in 1962. In 1981 the garden was bought by the fashion designer Yves St Laurent.

Jacques Majorelle travelled in the Atlas mountains and southern deserts and was struck by the Berber habit of outlining window frames and the interior of alcoves with a particular shade of deep, cobalt blue.

He bought a plot of land in 1924 and built a house and studio there, and in 1931 laid out the gardens and, significantly, painted the studio the Berber blue that he had seen in the Atlas mountains. This was then an extremely radical thing to do and provided a unique backdrop to Majorelle's collection of plants. He was an obsessive plant collector, financing plant-hunting expeditions and specialising in cacti and succulents and palms – all of which still dominate the garden.

As well as a bananas, cycads, jacarandas, sago and date palms, there are scores of hugely tall palms rocketing up free of the garden. This vertical structure transforms the space into something more than a collection of plants – into a tall plant cathedral with intense colours like stained glass. Despite this, the garden is curiously unspiritual. It is a garden of earthly delights rather than of the soul.

The hard landscaping has walls, paths and steps completed with a degree of permanence that is unusual in anything but the grandest gardens. This is what extreme wealth buys you in a garden: infrastructure. Plants come and go and can be quickly replaced. But to have the infrastructure of your garden built with exactly the same solidity as your house is true luxury. Garden writers and designers talk a lot about the 'bones' of a garden, but they are a fact as important as the cheekbones in a starlet's face. The better the bone structure the better the flesh sits.

There are over 300 pots in the garden planted beautifully with, in just one corner, *Strelitzia*, cordylines, citrus, cacti, aloes. They sit amongst various Buddhas and lovely garden furniture arched over with the fronds of the trees or set against the buildings. The effect is amazing.

The whole place has great restraint despite the exotic luxury. It has a real sense of style, and this gives it substance and strength. Susan has created a green refuge in the middle of the city entirely free from prying eyes – and opulent privacy is the greatest luxury in starstruck, crazy LA.

THE JIM THOMPSON HOUSE

BANGKOK, THAILAND

This was the home of the eponymous American entrepreneur who founded the Jim Thompson Thai Silk Company and built a house on one of the *Klongs* that run through Bangkok, right in the heart of the silk district. The house, which is set back from the street and surrounded by its garden, is an exquisite traditional wooden building, painted red, with steep tiled roofs. Inside, the wooden floors and walls are a burnished brown and the whole building is filled with paintings, prints, sculptures, porcelain, books and beautiful furniture. It is clearly the home of a wealthy aesthete and apparently still as he left it, meaning to return a few days later. The garden weaves around and even under the house, rising on various levels and with large trees screening out the city that presses in on three sides.

Jim Thompson finished the house in 1959 and disappeared after going for a walk in the jungle whilst on holiday in Malaya in 1967. The house and the garden that he made around it are open to the public and there is a restaurant and a shop selling the lovely silks that the company still makes. This little garden, lived in for only eight years by a foreigner, attracts as many visitors as Sissinghurst.

The garden is quite extraordinarily fulsome and lush and you cannot see through the undergrowth – which makes it seem much bigger than it actually is. However, it is not a traditional Thai garden. The Thai way is to clear the jungle and keep it away from the buildings, not least to try and reduce mosquitoes. Jim, the American in love with this exotic country, was creating his notion of Thailand from an assembly of buildings and an idea of a safe and domesticated jungle.

Hanging down by a path in long and absurdly unreal-looking festoons are the flower bracts of *Heliconia* (far left). It has banana-like leaves on tall stems and when the flowers open, like parading cockatoos, it becomes wholly surreal.

As in all Thai gardens, there is a small temple with floral offerings (left).

THE SITTA GARDEN

MOSMAN, NEW SOUTH WALES, AUSTRALIA

Truly contemporary 'designed' gardens are rare anywhere and they are always something of a shock. The risk is that all domesticity is submerged in the preciousness of fine art. This garden, in the fashionable suburb of Mosman, was designed by Vladimir Sitta, who self-consciously set out to capture what he described to me as "the burning red heart of the country" within the confines of this very small city space. It had also to house the owner's collection of succulent plants. The result is fiercely modern and challenging.

Sitta had 33 tons of red rock delivered from a quarry in Alice Springs. Now finished, hewn blocks of bright orange-red sandstone make walls with sharp corners rising up out of the ground like beached stone ships. The stone veers out of the ground with tectonic energy. In this tiny space this extends the garden down into the ground completing the walls as they disappear, making the garden somehow seem bigger conceptually if not spatially.

The owner's collection of succulents, hitherto always in pots, are planted in drifts within the small beds or planting pockets they contain, and gravelled areas seem to zigzag off from them, the angles jagging against each other. A grid of grey-blue *Festuca glauca* planted in the gravel nods towards a lawn.

The boundary is planted to provide a visual and weather screen using *Agave attenuata*, *Euphorbias*, *Echeveria*, *Aeonium atroprupurum* 'Schwartzkopf' and a large ponytail palm, *Beaucarnea recurvata*, whose water-storing roots hang from the three stems like solid tassels. Although there is a lot crammed into this small space and there is certainly not much room to kick a ball or have a barbie in, it does not feel crowded. On its own terms it feels right.

The result is a modern, urban garden that invites admiration and even awe, but perhaps not the slow affection of a garden that evolves and adapts with its gardener.

LONGHOUSE RESERVE

EAST HAMPTON, NEW YORK, USA

Longhouse Reserve is the home of the weaver Jack Larson and the house, set in 16 acres of land in East Hampton, was intended from the outset as a place to display works of art of all kinds. It is a permanent gallery that houses an eclectic, changing and always very personal choice of art. Larson began the project sixteen years ago when he was already sixty-five. This seems to me to epitomise the indominable spirit of optimism and willingness to embrace the new that typifies all that is best about American culture.

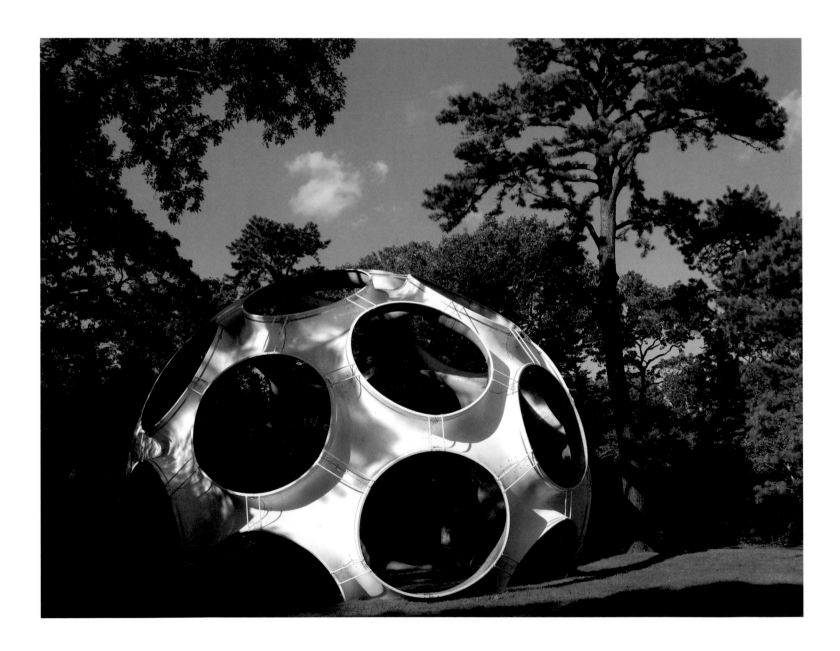

Sculpture set in a garden or designed landscape challenges the way that we look at both gardens and art. Both can sit uneasily with each other and become self-conscious and even diminished by the intrusion of the other. But when they do work together something greater than the sum of the parts, horticultural and artistic, is reached. Many of the artworks in this garden derive from natural forms and echo them in shape, style or texture. Others (opposite) challenge the organic growth around them with hard, mechanistic form

The Red Garden (opposite) has a grass path flanked by cloud-pruned azaleas, assuredly red in flower, and spaced along both hedges are eleven pairs of red uprights made from brightly painted sections of tree trunks, complete with all the knots and gnarls that make them tree-like rather than post-like. These diminish in size and become closer together as they approach the end, which is marked by a sculpture by Toshiko Takaezen that looks like a pot or a stone but is neither. It is just its ceramic self. The simplicity of all of this and the containment, the inevitability of it, makes it work both as garden and as art.

The house (top right) is modelled upon upon a Shinto shrine at Ise in Japan.

Having tree-like sculpture next to trees makes you look at the organic forms as sculpture and vice versa. When the boundary between garden and sculpture becomes blurred, with beautifully pruned trees and sculptures made from wood or ceramics that look like tree trunks, the place comes alive in a very idiosyncratic way.

A small grass amphitheatre like a Celtic hill fort (bottom right), slightly concave, is a lovely green space. It seems that it was born of the practical need to dispose of the soil that was excavated to make the pond, but it is none the less pleasing for this. It is the perfect synthesis of sculpture and horticulture.

THE ROCK GARDEN
MAGDALESBERG, GAUTENG, SOUTH AFRICA

This was the last garden that I visited on my journey round the world and it remains one of my favourites. It consists of two acres set in a further 90 of – as yet – untouched hillside. Geoffrey Armstrong is a sculptor and his partner Wendy, a painter and printer. The house and garden are a seamless part of their life and work. It is common enough to see works of art placed within and as part of a garden, and quite frequently artists make excellent gardeners, but it is very rare that the garden itself transcends these distinctions and becomes the artwork itself. This garden is unequivocally a superb work of art.

The garden is entirely constructed from stone, wood, water and plants. The hillside has been excavated, burrowed and moulded by pick and shovel and then carefully arranged and embellished. Rocks are used where trees, hedges or shrubs might be expected in many gardens. They pile on top of each other, lean, poise, balance, peer and pose like courtiers in attendance. Every single one of tens, hundreds of thousands of these stones, from the smallest pebble to the huge monoliths, have been carefully positioned by Geoffrey. The wood has all been carved by him.

Geoffrey and Wendy go on rescue collections, gathering
plants from the path of roads or buildings in virgin
country much as Burle Marx did in Brazil, and then
they come back with a mass of plants that have to be
planted in order that they might survive. So a new space
is cleared and carved out – often literally – for them.
Mainly grasses, agaves, aloes and other succulents with
the occasional exclamation of colour, the plants people
the garden, and give it a warmth that mitigates the
underlying severity of Geoffrey's vision.

Water is a key feature of the garden, running through rock channels, carved wooden pipes and conduits into a series of pools. The combination of the dry orange rock and the mass of succulent plants with so much water increases the surrealism of the garden.

The natural slope of the hillside has been gauged and hollowed like one of Geoffrey's sculptures – it is one of his sculptures – so ravines, hillocks and rocky passes leading nowhere map this new made-up land. Wooden bowls, boulders and bony carcasses jostle the stone until they marry into a kind of composite, organic material. There are no paths – or if there seem to be paths then they are usurped and invaded by new developments, nipping their progress in the bud. Huge wooden constructs, walkways, viewing platforms, jutting piers of plank all echo the rhythms of the trees.

It is a garden that enlarges and transcends the limitations of horticulture and yet has a huge and lovingly tended range of plants. Above all, despite its freedom as a work of art, it is a garden rooted deep in the ground of the place, created in the rock, flora and soil of Magdalesberg and out of the vision and loving expertise of two superb artists.

THE ROCK GARDEN
CHANDIGARH, PUNJAB, INDIA

The rock garden at Chandigarh was made in secret by one man, Nek Shand, working entirely unaided over eighteen years. To make the new town of Chandigarh, after partition, more than twenty villages were cleared, creating a huge amount of rubble and waste. In 1953 Shand began to collect bits and pieces of this rubble – broken plates, light fittings, door handles, stones, tiles, anything at all – and take them on his bicycle to the small clearing that he had found in the jungle. He did not own the land, nor did anyone else know he was creating this eccentric garden. By 1971 when it was finally discovered, Nek had covered acres of ground with hundreds of sculptures set in twisting paths, waterways and rock faces. To their eternal credit, the local authorities not only decided to keep it but gave Nek a salary to work on it, plus 50 labourers to assist him. In 1976 it was formally inaugurated as The Rock Garden of Chandigarh and the world began to take in the immensity of what had secretly and quietly been created. The garden now runs to 25 acres and is visited by nearly two million people a year. It has been acclaimed as the greatest artistic achievement in India since the Taj Mahal.

The garden is a series of tableaux or fantasies constructed entirely from found objects. Pieces of found stone worn into shapes that Nek liked are set alongside others that he has constructed. There is no division between natural objects and wholly fanciful ones. No rules. No boundaries. Pipes made from concrete writhe out of a wall like a mass of beautiful tree roots. Above this, a real tree grows directly out of the wall. What could be catacombs are cut into the rock and fronted with carved hieroglyphs. Water cascades down a green, mossy bank within a gorge. Little houses perch on the rocks above. There is a simple wall of ceramic insulators topped with tiny terracotta pots threaded on wire like beads on an abacus. There is no question of taste or style or design or intention to please.

Although it is the work of an artist that has rare genius, Nek Shand has never owned it nor sold any part of his work. That purity of vision and spirit flows through the place and makes visiting it a curiously moving spiritual experience.

Carry on round corners, down steps, squeezing through narrow stone passageways and you come to a series of spaces populated by animals and people, hundreds and hundreds of them, each one modelled out of terracotta or concrete and embellished with broken pottery, pebbles or glass beads. They make an army whose massed effect is incredibly haunting and yet each one is different, a sculpture in its own right that rivals the work of Míro or Picasso – although I suspect that Nek Shand had barely heard of these two when he made them.

All these figures seem to represent India as surely and accurately as the music, temples and myriad other signifiers of this extraordinary country. Broken plates, clinker, stone and the waste from a new town are all made into works of art that are filled with humanity and an uncanny portrait of modern India.

THE GARDEN VINEYARD

THE MORNINGTON PENINSULA, VICTORIA, AUSTRALIA

The Garden Vineyard – or Fusion Garden as it is also and more descriptively known – is a journey through the assimilation of Australia by Di Johnson, an Englishwoman, working as a GP and bringing up her very Australian children, but homesick for the England of her childhood and especially for its countryside. The garden is a progression through her life and the fusion is of two cultures and floras set on the opposite sides of the earth. It begins with a very English tableau and arrives at a garden dedicated to native Australian species. The result is idiosyncratically Australian and the expression of a native Australian horticulture that reflects its colonial journey in a way that perhaps only an outsider could portray.

A grass path curves between a pair of huge borders in an early section of the garden. They are made up from 650 cubic yards of topsoil bought in by Di, sight unseen, just as the planting is 'bought in'. Although Di was moving towards an assimilation of British and Australian styles when she made these borders, by her own account, they are strongly influenced by Beth Chatto and a very English style, with great drifts of penstemons, knifophia, salvias, dahlias, *Alchemilla mollis*, opium poppies, cardoons and dozen more plants from a standard English plant list. But the clipped columns that add structure to the border turn out to be lillypilly (*Acmena smithii var. minor*), which is native to Australia. Di says that they take the heat and dryness completely in their stride. However the very British lushness of the mown grass is only possible with heavy watering.

Making the garden was, for Di, a process of applying Alexander Pope's famous horticultural dictum and "consulting the genius of the place". Gradually she realised that her longing for a traditional English garden would translate into something more creative, with a restricted range of plants and palette of colours, yet which was just as beautiful. She skilfully combines tightly clipped native plants with billowing grasses and herbaceous perrenials to build a rhythm of delicate colours and scultpural shapes that flows right through the garden.

From the flanking borders filled with half Australian and half British planting you turn a sharp corner and arrive at an area composed of perfectly clipped balls and mounds of lillypilly, glabra, *Rhagodia spinescens*, grey *Westringia fruticosa* (a rosemary-like shrub with 25 species native to Australia), lavender and a round white-trunked lemon-scented eucalyptus (opposite). Paddock grass grows in the open space. The colours are muted to greys, ochres (including all the grass), and largely glaucous shades of green. Unlike the borders, this part of the garden is hardly ever watered as these are all native and Mediterranean species perfectly adapted to the fiercely hot, dry climate. In the outback these plants are loose, almost meadow-like, but the tight, sculptural clipping of the naturally scraggy native plants transforms them. Surely this is the definition of gardening?

At the centre, the garden then moves into a large, very European, formal area of garden made of lillypilly lollypops flanking broad formal paths (right). The coppery lillypilly is underplanted with vast stretches of white agapanthus and heliotrope bedding. This is formal grandeur on a scale that is breathtaking in a private garden.

AYRLIES

AUCKLAND, NEW ZEALAND

This is a garden that submerses the visitor in plants, dunks and wallows you in their colour, texture, shape and scent. It is twelve acres of garden and another 30 acres of woodland, but it seems much bigger than that because of the scale and sheer intensity of its planting. Ayrlies is just 40 years old but astonishingly mature. The trees are huge and the whole garden timelessly established. It is hard to believe that in 1964 this was just a series of empty grass paddocks for dairy cattle. The garden was created by and is still lived in and run by Beverley McConnell, the doyenne of New Zealand gardening and plantsperson in the great tradition of Christopher Lloyd or Beth Chatto.

There are scores of different islands of plant groups more or less interlinked via paths, ponds, gushing streams, steep steps and lawns, but it is clear that design is secondary to the plants. Glowing in the astonishingly clear New Zealand light, the planting is ecstatic. There are no straight lines and few obvious directional routes. You wander or, more accurately, dive into depths of light and colour.

When Beverley and her husband came to Ayrlies in 1964 the farm was hilly pasture – like most of the southern part of North Island – and a working dairy farm. There was no garden. Beverley says "I married a man who thought big. In those days a lot of farmers would say to their wives if they wanted to make a garden 'What do you want to do that for?', but my husband would always say 'Why not?'. Gardens eat money but he wrote the cheques. We planted every single tree here. That first three acres stayed for about ten years. Then we went to England and on that trip my husband saw water gardens for the first time and wanted it here. We came back and there was a local man that needed work so my husband got him to dig four ponds. So the garden automatically increased to about 10 or 12 acres."

These 12 acres grow at a race. There is nearly 50 inches of rain a year, the weather is never too cold, never too hot and there are 365 growing days a year. However, this means that there are hardly any herbaceous plants as they do not have the dormant period that they need.

I ask Beverely what advice she would give to anyone setting out to make a large garden. Her response: "Plant your trees and give them ten years to establish. Then get your water established. Then infill it with plants. Create your own nursery to raise plants and above all, prepare the ground well."

At every turn of the twelve acres of intensively planted garden you meet surprise and delight. Ayrlies transcends the good taste and horticultural confidence that is typical of so many of Europe's grand gardens. It makes you look anew. I have never seen such a wide mixture of plants in one garden and I have never seen colour and plant association handled better or sustained with such intensity on such a scale.

2

Ryoan-ji
Isshidan
Ryugintei
ToteKiKo
Urasenke
Tofukuji
The Humble Administrator's Garden
The Lion Grove Garden
The Taj Mahal
Jal Mahal
Akbar's Tomb
Pura Taman Ayun

SPIRITUAL

Spirituality quickly founders on the rocks of language. Poetry can come to the rescue but reason and intellect are usually little help. When the languages involved are unfamiliar and frustratingly inaccessible it is easy to find yourself struggling to express the extent to which you are failing to articulate. This was the position that I found myself in regarding Eastern religions. So when travelling to the Far East I deliberately sought out gardens that might elucidate the spiritual inarticulateness that I felt entangled in. I wanted intellectual explanation through the medium of horticulture, but also knew that the gardens themselves were so interwoven in the spiritual lives of their makers and carers that they might be the key to their spiritual centre. I travelled to India, Indonesia, China and Japan, pursuing the mingled threads of Buddhism, Islam, Hinduism, Confucionism and Shinto. History, anthropology and ritual are all clearly essential components of these religions and cultures that find many expressions in their gardens, but at the heart of all of them is something less definable and yet more enduringly powerful. I discovered, as so many have before me, that their gardens were not only a profound way to enter the spirituality of the culture – but also that of my own spirit.

RYOAN-JI

KYOTO, JAPAN

Ryoan-ji is the most famous and one of the oldest of Kyoto's thousands of Zen temple gardens. The present garden was made in 1499, although a temple had been on the site for 500 years previously. It is one of the world's great gardens yet is very small – 30 feet by 100 – and consists of just fifteen rocks in four groups, each surrounded by a small pool of moss and set in raked gravel, enclosed on two sides by a wall with a deeply pitched and tiled capping, on one side by a temple building and on the fourth a newer wall and small building. That's it. Nothing much at all. Just rocks, gravel and moss arranged flawlessly and great unfathomable pools of space.

There are many explanations and theories about the precise 'meaning' of each group of stones, from islands to tiger cubs crossing a sea to magical numerical theory. That they are heavy with significance is instantly apparent. What they mean seems to limit them rather than explain.

The buildings and their very simple details are as much an essential part of the garden as the garden is of the temple. One side of the temple opens via the veranda directly onto the garden and you can only see the garden from that elevated space. The garden and building are all of a piece – the colour of the wood is exactly that of the tiles coping the enclosing wall; the paint of the walls can best be described as raked gravel colour; the golden, weather-stained garden wall is the colour of the mats on the floor of the open rooms. Every tiny detail is exact and connected with a meaningful, yet gossamer, thread.

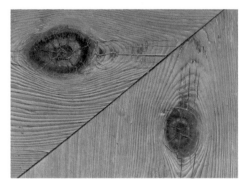

ISSHIDAN
RYOGEN-IN, DAITOKUJI COMPOUND, KYOTO, JAPAN

Isshidan is one of the five gardens that are part of the temple of Ryogen-in, which in turn is part of the huge Daitokuji temple complex in Kyoto. These five gardens interact and should be seen as a group, but each is a wholly separate entity. The original garden dates from 1505 when the temple was completed, but it was substantially remade in 1980 when its main tree, which was over 700 years old, died. This modernity is an essential element in the very traditional setting and culture. It is more than just a careful historical remodelling or reconstruction. It is a new work in its own right and yet seamlessly fitting into a historical monument and style.

Isshidan is superficially similar to Ryoan-ji in that there is an earth-coloured clay wall capped with tiles, painted ochre, groups of stones set in raked gravel and moss and the temple along one of the long sides. But the atmosphere is very different and on closer inspection, the elements are handled in a dramatically different way. In a gardening idiom where every tiny detail counts – and is counted by every visitor – this makes for dynamic changes.

Everything about it is more muscular and imposing than Ryoan-ji. The white gravel (it is in fact a particularly sticky, stony river sand) representing the sea is raked into much more vigorous and deep rills with clear dividing lines like low banks marking them out. The stones are bigger and the moss more obviously delineated. You are also more aware of the neighbouring buildings rather than the trees that are the sole backdrop to Ryoan-ji.

Despite the proximity of neighbouring temples the garden feels open and unrestrained. It has a kind of active calm.

Whereas Ryoan-ji is open to many different kinds of interpreation, Isshidan is clearly figurative with the three groups stones and moss representing a *kameshima* or tortoise island, a *tsurushima* or crane island and the large stones in the middle representing Mount Horai. The tortoise and crane are both symbols of long life and happiness in Japanese culture – the crane because it takes the crane a thousand years to fly to the sun and the tortoise because it does not grow a tail until it is 500 years old. Mount Horai is the mythological group of mountains where the ancient, and immortal, Chinese sages are supposed to have lived.

There are twelve wells in the garden, some for drinking, some for damping paths and some for watering plants. The best well has the purest water, which can only be collected at the 'best' time. In line with everything in the gardens, the buckets are simply – but elegantly – made from bamboo and stored neatly and precisely in an exact manner.

This, like all tea gardens, is divided into an outer and an inner garden. Between the two is a middle gate where my host – the Grand Master Zabosai Soshitsu Sen XVI – comes and greets me before taking me to the tea room. In fact, over the centuries each grand master would build a new tea house, so now there are thirteen, each with its own tiny dedicated garden, and Urasenke mazes around them. Paths that are not to be followed are marked by a rock tied by thick black twine. They alone, on their stepping stone and surrounded by moss, are works of elegant art.

The Japanese revere the old and yet easily embrace the modern. In some ways this is reflected in their gardens – old plants inevitably pruned to the inch and held in a taut dynamic of longevity and renewal.

TOFUKUJI

KYOTO, JAPAN

Tofukuji is the head temple of the Rinzai sect of Zen Buddhism. The original building was built in 1236 but was rebuilt in the fifteenth century after a fire and it remains one of the great surviving medieval temples in Kyoto. However, the garden, made in 1939 by Mirei Shigemori, is one of the great modern, even revolutionary, gardens of Japan.

Shigemori was steeped in the traditions of Zen temple gardens. He wanted to create something that was new and related to idioms of the twentieth century and yet not to lose any of the traditional elements.

As with most temple gardens it revolves around a central Abbots Hall as a series of separate but linked gardens reflecting the eight thoughts of the Buddha. At the back of the building there is – to my eyes – the great masterpiece of this garden and perhaps of all horticulture (opposite). A chequer-board theme moves from clipped azaleas to moss, with stone making up the other part of the pattern. As the squares move on along the building as part of the sixth thought of Buddha, they seem to dissolve and float away with the moss becoming closer together, the stone disappearing and, with incredible attention to detail and skill, the moss itself becoming shorter, thinner and sparser until that too more or less fades away into gravel. This is genius.

This is followed (left) by a garden of the constellations where traditional stones are replaced by seven carved stones (originally foundation stones of the former temple building), representing the main stars of Ursa Major in gravel which again merges into moss with trees and a clipped hedge.

The first part of Shigemori's design is a large dry gravel and stone garden. Although to the uninformed Western eye this garden seems familiar and conventional, it created a huge stir. The Abbot and the monks accepted and understood it, but many of the public hated it and there was a huge outcry. The garden was vilified because it was thought that it introduced Western techniques into sacred temple space. The stones are huge – modern cranes and transport made this possible – and unusually numerous and, most shocking of all to the traditionalists, many are lying on their sides instead of vertically. This might seem slight, but it had never been done before.

This large garden represents four islands or changes or thoughts and four phases of the garden, going from stone through changes as it moves down to the other end of the hall, the stones giving way to five mounds or islands of moss. Like the stones these mounds are distinctly larger than in other Zen gardens, almost real islands with a bonsai pine at their centre.

THE HUMBLE ADMINISTRATOR'S GARDEN

SUZHOU, JIANGSU PROVINCE, CHINA

During the reign of the emperor Zhengde, between 1506 and 1521, the site of what is now the Humble Administrators Garden in Suzhou was occupied by a Dahong Temple. This was appropriated by a tax collector called Wang Xianchen, who turned it into a private villa with a garden – and what remains today is an amalgam built around the core of the early-sixteenth-century garden. About 100 years after it was built, at the end of the Ming Dynasty (1368–1650), it was divided up into three sections, with the western and central parts becoming villas of government officials. However, when the Ming Dynasty was replaced by the Qing Dynasty the garden was repaired and especially in the early years of the eighteenth century there were extensive modifications. About 70 years later, under the emperor Qianlong, the garden was divided into two parts, and what the modern visitor sees is essentially this late Qing stage of the garden, although it was not until 1949 that the eastern portion was joined to the centre.

The walls are all white and topped with beautifully tiled roofs over walkways or just as capping. The colour of the tiles signifies rank – with yellow used for imperial palaces and temples, green for princes and grey for humility.

Nature is distilled constantly in search of its essence. Every branch of every tree is shaped, considered and artfully trained so that it seems to have arrived at this moment entirely by chance. Confucionism teaches order and duty, Taoism simplicity and restraint. Both of these huge philosophies are to be found in a single branch in the Chinese garden.

All walls have lattice openings through which you can glimpse the view ahead. Every style of lattice has meaning – or so I am told. It is like walking through the streets of Suzhou, a babble of speech in an entirely strange tongue. There is nothing for it but to let the mind go and just take it in.

Everything is to be glimpsed. Everything is framed or set against a backdrop to create a complete tableau or picture – even if this is tiny or very simple.

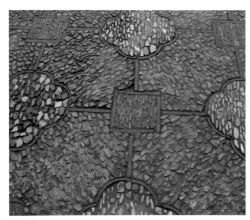

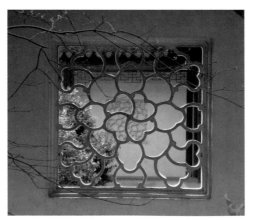

Huge stones are set like sculptures along the way, the more holes and contortions the better. There are far more rocks than plants and they are tended with the same care as the rarest specimen in a botanical garden. Rocks are revered. One man apparently adopted one as his brother.

The paths that we race along are in themselves wonderful, all mosaiced stone with a deceptively simple intricacy.

There is more water than land and the paths negotiate the ponds like a maze. Like Suzhou itself, with its labyrinth of canals, this is a garden of buildings buttressed by water.

Rocks are Yang and must be balanced by the Yin of water. So the rocky maze that the visitor wanders through ends at an open pool banked by tiers of these rocks doubling themselves in the black water. The stones are all individuals. The effect is massed but, as ever, nothing is casual. Each one is carefully chosen.

THE LION GROVE GARDEN
SUZHOU, JIANGSU PROVINCE, CHINA

The Lion Grove Garden was originally created in 1342 by a monk, Weize, who wished to create a garden to remind himself of his former home, the Lion Rock on Tianmu mountain. Apparently Weize's teacher rode a lion to the site of the garden, where it lay down and refused to move. When it shook its mane the hairs flew out and when they touched the ground each one turned into a lion cub. Now gnarled, pitted, holed and contorted rocks pile on top of each other at every turn and every one is supposed to suggest a lion or some part of its anatomy.

All the stones in this garden come from nearby Lake Taiu and were particularly prized for their holes. The chemical composition of the lake eroded the limestone irregularly, thus creating the fantastic shapes and the uniform grey colouring of the stone.

Against each wall are set narrow borders of stones and bamboo to create idealised landscapes, the whitewash of the walls is particularly prized for the stains, fading paint and mould that is all encouraged as part of the composition.

A quatrefoil doorway (bottom right) frames a stone shaped like a lion's head.

THE TAJ MAHAL
AGRA, UTTAR PRADESH, INDIA

The Taj Mahal is one of the most recognisable and revered buildings on earth, yet many people do not realise that it was built between 1631 and 1654 as a tomb for Mumtaz Mahal, the dead wife of the Mogul emperor Shah Jahan, and that the garden was created as an integral part of the monument. It was a Paradise garden and Shah Jahan intended the Taj Mahal to be an earthly replica of the house and garden that Mumtaz was now inhabiting.

The Taj Mahal was, on one level, another river-front garden in a well-established and distinguished tradition. Agra was a city of gardens built since the Moguls made it their capital of Hindustan in 1526, all fronting both sides of the river Yamuna. The garden was of central significance in the Mogul world and it would have been unthinkable for the Taj Mahal not to have been set in its own *chahar bagh*, the quartered garden that inevitably included water in rills, fountains and tanks, and orchards filled with fruit.

Recent archeology has revealed that the tomb is set in the middle of the garden, with the river dividing the two halves. The newly discovered half on the far side of the river is gradually being uncovered and replanted.

JAL MAHAL
JAIPUR, RAJASTHAN, INDIA

Just outside the old city of Jaipur is an extraordinary garden in the process of complete restoration. This is Jal Mahal, which was originally built as a pleasure garden in 1725 by the Maharajah of Jaipur, Jai Singh, who had his principal palace on the hillside above it. It is a garden housed within a building that is set in the middle of a vast lake. The garden is on the top floor of this building, which from a distance appears to be a palace but which actually exists simply to support the weight of the soil and pavilions set around the outside. On three sides are hills, with the honey-coloured stone of the Maharajah's palatial pavilions across the water. The Maharajah would send word that he was coming and servants would put down the carpets, set out lights, prepare food, and he would come with his guests and stay perhaps for one evening, perhaps for a week or two, just to relax. They might have dancing, fireworks and wonderful food. It was a garden dedicated to pleasure.

When I visited, the lake was dry and the building stranded in hundreds of acres of sand being grazed by cattle. We walked across the dry lake bed to it. But when the monsoon comes the lake rapidly fills and the garden can only be approached by boat.

Upon the roof of the building is the garden, also a building site but with large trees and eight pavilions – placed at each corner and centrally around the sides. In the centre is a fountain and raised walkway above the quartered format of a *chahar bagh*. I watched as ten men carefully placed cinerarias in pots within the arabesque scrolling of white plastered stone. The plan is to have the garden predominately white. White jasmine, white poppies, white bougainvillea and white wisteria.

As the women gracefully carried the bowls of mortar up and down the stairs and across the garden site, scores of people were at work, including a team of four stone carvers squatting under the sun chipping delicately at blocks of white marble.

The restoration work is meticulous, with the stone gathered from the same quarry as the original and the workmen directly descended from the artisans that made the Taj Mahal – and the same skills have been passed in an unbroken line down the generations through the centuries.

AKBAR'S TOMB

SIKANDRA, UTTAR PRADESH, INDIA

Jalaluddin Muhammad Akbar was the grandson of the great Babur, the first Mogul emperor, who ruled from 1508 to 1530, invading India from his capital in Kabul in 1518 and bringing with him the Persian garden plan *chahar bagh*. Akbar ruled from 1556 to 1605 and was the greatest of the Moguls. His tomb is centred in the middle of a vast garden completely enclosed within high stone walls. The whole thing is at least twice the size of the much more celebrated Taj Mahal. Like all Persian gardens it is divided into four equal squares, two of which are likewise quartered again.

The earliest Persian gardens, dating back to 2000 BC, were known as *chahar bagh*, or fourfold garden, which reflected the importance of the four sacred elements and the division of the world into four equal segments, with a spring of life at its centre. The divisions were not marked by paths, as in western courtyard gardens, but by water channels meeting at a central pool or fountain.

When I was there the water channels were dry, which felt both a pity and a travesty – although at a time of drought I could see that there were other more vital calls upon available water supplies. But to see the garden as intended it should be dominated by its water.

The gentle sound of overflowing water, as it moved around the channels and fountains, was an essential component of the original garden.

The Paradise gardens of the Moguls would invariably contain fruit and animals – and, very unusually, Akbar's tomb still houses a menagerie of deer, peacocks and monkeys within the garden walls.

PURA TAMAN AYUN

UBUD, BALI

Pura Taman Ayun ('the beautiful palace garden') was built in 1634 as part of the capital of the ancient kingdom of Mengwi. The Temple is divided into three sections, outer, middle and inner (below). The visitor cannot go into the inner sanctum, but there is a path right the way round and a low wall with a moat in front of it and looked over this to a series of shrines with tiered thatched roofs. They make a staggeringly beautiful succession of outlines against the sky, the thatch black and lined like the underside of a field mushroom. The size of the shrines indicated their status – each one has an odd number of tiers, with eleven the most important of them all.

A huge terracotta brick-and-stone gateway covered in carvings of gods and demons is the entrance to the inner part. These doors are only opened for ceremonies that take place every 21 days and every full and new moon.

All the shrines are made of sandstone, wood and reeds. Nothing is painted or embellished, although the carvings and outlines are fabulously ornate. The essence of these Balinese temples is to preserve a natural simplicity with tranquillity and serenity through choice of materials. The carvings on all the shrines are apparently done after they are built, carving into the building itself rather than assembling it. What they aspire to is authenticity rather than sincerity.

Overleaf: Lotus flowers in the moat surrounding the inner sanctum.

Juan Grimm's Garden
James van Sweden's Garden
Alice Springs Desert Park
Te Kainga Marire
Villa Bebek: Made Wijaya's Garden
The Black Earth

NATURAL

All gardens are, by definition, unnatural. They impose order and restraint upon the natural world, however lightly this control is worn. But whereas some gardens are formal and delight in the constraints that they create and maintain, others try and work with nature to establish a harmony. In other words they let the prevailing conditions of climate, geography, geology and botany limit the scope and style of the garden. In my travels around the world I became increasingly interested in and impressed by gardens that limited themselves to indigenous plants. This goes against the grain of prevailing Western horticultural tradition, which prides itself on the accumulaton of as varied and wide-ranging a plant collection as possible – usually as an expression of past colonial domination. But the following gardens work much more sympathetically and subtly than that, creating stunning spaces that celebrate their local limitations.

JUAN GRIMM'S GARDEN
LOS VILLOS, SANTIAGO, CHILE

Juan Grimm is one of the world's leading landscape and garden designers and his house and garden – both designed by himself – are in a stunningly spectacular location overlooking the Pacific at Los Villos. As with all his work, public and private, this garden integrates the controlling hand of man with the natural landscape and plants with breathtaking subtlety and skill. His garden starts literally at the water's edge and runs up to the house. The planting does not turn away from the sea but embraces it and uses the rocks and even the waves as part of the whole. The result is one of the most beautiful and inspiring gardens anywhere in the world.

The approach to the house is almost entirely green, with the house itself tucked into this verdancy as a series of boxes broken by a huge stone wall. The sea is hidden. The green flows and swells like cloud topiary, a kind of tightly controlled bubbling of foliage. But as soon as you enter the building and look out, that greenness is overpowered by the blue of sea and sky.

The spiky leaves of a silvery *Puya* (below) are topped with artichoke-like heads bursting with violet flowers like electric pineapples.

Juan's garden was inspired by his visits as a child to the coast some ten miles south. So all the plants on the seaward side of the garden are not just native to Chile but to that specific area of Los Molles.

The garden challenges horticulture. Where does it begin and end? Is the lichen gardening? The rock pools? The pebbles washed up by the sea or even the drying tide on the rocks?

The plants on the rocks and around the rock pools near the sea are all natural. But Juan waters them all throughout the six baking, dry Chilean summer months and this encourages extra germination and growth. So the bromeliads, cacti and astrolerias thrive and flower on the bare rocks. He moves plants – and stones and driftwood – and weeds and cuts the grasses back to stop them predominating.

The genius is in the subtle gradation from shore to threshold, the garden evolving from water and encrusted rock to sleek modernity without ever missing a beat or betraying the spirit of that particular coastline. Gradually the rocks become covered by vegetation as you move away from the shore towards the house, although the progresssion is seamless. Juan told me that he wanted the house to be like just another rock and every few years it is painted black to exactly match the colour of the lichen tidemark.

The swimming pool is a circle edged with wooden boards, like a hole dropping down into the ocean.

JAMES VAN SWEDEN'S GARDEN

CHESAPEAKE BAY, MARYLAND, USA

The garden of the leading American garden designer James Van Sweden looks out over the Atlantic at Chesapeake Bay and is based upon indigenous prairie grasses requiring minimal maintenance. It is stylish and even dramatic, yet it merges into the landscape without a break in its stride. This, especially in the USA, is revolutionary gardening.

Van Sweden told me that he wanted the house to be floating in a meadow like the ones in Michigan where he grew up. So all the grasses used in the garden are native and the garden is based around grasses. He uses mass planting – "up to 1,000 of each plant" and lays the plants out and only then cuts pathways through them. This is a novel and brilliantly simple way of establishing natural paths and defining planting areas with natural planting. There is, he assures me, practically no maintenance at all.

Underlying the apparent artlessness is great skill and he has used a wide and extensive range of plants to create the natural effect. Flanking the path to the front door were great stands, perhaps hundreds strong, of *Rudbeckia, Aster, Eupatorium, Inula* and *Helenium* amongst others. It was as though he had taken the idea of a flower border, shaken it up and set it down with all the pretension and preciousness taken from it.

The house is skirted by bleached pine decking, salted and weathered to the same tone as the sand and the grasses and driftwood. All the chairs and tables on the deck are made out of sun-bleached driftwood, as is the palisade-like gazebo down by the water's edge. The more you look the more you realise that every detail has been stripped from intrusion and pretension and yet involves design and careful horticulture as much as any formal garden.

By using indigenous plants and embracing the flowing natural grasses of the prairie James van Sweden seems to have touched the nerve of what American gardens could be, using indigenous species, without aping European ideas, and whilst being sustainable in a slowly cooking world.

ALICE SPRINGS DESERT PARK

NORTHERN TERRITORY, AUSTRALIA

I had been told, in Sydney, that rural Australia is too harsh and too dominant to make a garden. But the Alice Springs Desert Park disproves this with its use of native plants and the way that it delights in the harshness of the baking interior of the continent. It is a 125-acre site that at first appears completely natural and untouched by man – no more a 'garden' than a patch of shore. But every detail is planted, landscaped and man-made. The intention was to combine all the elements of the desert and pull them together in one place. Having visited the Desert Park I am sure that my Sydney commentator was wrong. The future of Australia is being told out there, through its gardens in the burning heart of the country, as much as in the cities.

The salt lakes and clay pans showing only the salty ghost of water (opposite) are made as carefully any garden pond – and using almost identical techniques.

The park has flora and a lot of fauna in beautifully designed and integrated buildings along the route, from all the different recognised outback environments, Range, Gorge, the low scrub of Mulga Woodland, Desert Woodland, Desert Rivers and Sand Country.

Spinifex dominates the Sand Country. This grassy plant has twelve or so different species but all can grow in virtually phosphorous- and nitrogen-free soils and have deep roots that survive extreme drought. The leaves look soft and grassy but are in fact curled up spikes.

Despite the attention to every detail, clear labelling and subtle plant groupings and associations, it all feels entirely spontaneous. There is that sense you have in all good outdoor spaces that it would be worse if it were different.

Woods of large gums stand bare-barked and peeling, shimmering in the heat.

Plants are carefully encouraged to behave as they do when untended. So there are dead and fallen trees, and some blasted by lightening making charred sculptures as beautiful as a David Nash.

Very few people understand how complex and subtle the outback is and how sophisticated the Aboriginal management and use of it. Seeing it as just hostile desert to be subdued is blunt and ignorant.

The local Arrente people held this landscape of the park as very significant and it includes parts of the Wild Dog and Caterpillar dreaming stories. Dreamtime exists inside the landscape; it is part of it. These cannot be changed or altered without ripping away tens of thousands of years of cultural history. Nothing in the outback is without significance for them. To alter it in any way is to alter the dream stories and a real desecration. This adds a layer of meaning to the park that is profoundly important.

TE KAINGA MARIRE

NEW PLYMOUTH, NEW ZEALAND

Te Kainga Marire belongs to Valda Poletti and Dave Clarkson, who have been making the garden there since 1972. It is small, homely and based upon a wide range of indigenous plants. It is, in every sense, a modern New Zealand garden – friendly, beautiful and proud of its heritage.

The half-acre garden is divided into a series of areas that flow into each other seamlessly, making it seem larger than it is. It is essentially a suburban plot, part of a housing estate in New Plymouth, that embraces and absorbs the rainforest with its diversity of plants and extraordinary fecundity. It is an unexpected combination but it works with easy charm.

Dead trunks of tree ferns form a pillared approach to a low hut. Live tree ferns sprout above on their compressed stems of root. The temperate rainforest, of which the tree fern is the emerald jewel, is the greenest, most unthreateningly beautiful natural environment I have visited. This garden captures its benign magic perfectly.

The garden was made from ficus swamp (rappo) that had been dumped with clay. It was hardly an auspicious start. But Dave and Valda tended it during evenings and weekends whilst both working seven days a week. Every plant you see now, every tree, every aspect of landscaping has been planted or built by their own hands. The result is a very personal garden filled with a thousand details of their lives. Yet it is not introverted. As well as opening to the public (to whom they issue a magnifying glass to view the hidden details of plants) it is open to the big idea of New Zealand. It is a celebration of all that the country can grow, And that is a very great deal. Dave told me that they have 70-odd inches of rainfall a year and although they do get frosts half a dozen days a year, the growing season is twelve months. It never gets too hot and the rain is spread evenly so there is no dry season. "Visitors can't believe how fast everything grows here."

VILLA BEBEK: MADE WIJAYA'S GARDEN

SANUR, BALI

Made Wijaya is a flamboyant, erudite, complicated, articulate, outrageous man and completely dedicated to Bali and Balinese culture. The garden is ornate, crowded, intense, loaded with textures, fragrances, shapes, colours – although inevitably green dominates – and yet rather than being claustrophobic this feels of a piece with the lushness and intensity of light, heat and the underlying jungle waiting to return and engulf everything. Made Wijaya's brilliance is to understand the seething fecundity of that growth, ally it to the culture and traditions of the Balinese temple and compound gardens and create something modern and original from it.

Made Wijaya's garden at Villa Bebek is a performance, and a very self-conscious, self-confident one where every detail works towards the desired effect. These details accumulate relentlessly and are invariably loaded with wit, charm and a sense of playfulness. In the course of a long conversation, he told me how the garden was concieved.

"I was very influenced by the wild colours, the fecundity and the peopling of the gardens with these wild shrines and things. So I have tried to edit out the Dutch colonial influence of gentrification and use the natural garden styles without making it too kitschy or Disneyfied. You have to retain that spiritual element."

"This is a testing ground for various ideas. I wanted this to be a little mini history of all Bali trends. So I had water features I had seen in the palaces of East Bali, I have a sand garden, I have tried to collect ornamental courtyard trees and shrubs so it is a sort of museum of Balinese garden traditions. There are twelve pavilions and 48 different courtyards."

All this is crammed into a relatively small space. How does he do it?

"A small garden just requires a big idea. It is no easier to do a small courtyard. If you have pavilions in a compound you end up with lots of different spaces."

"Things are often in pots because they have lots of ceremonies and they have to move things round. Any good tropical architecture allows itself to be thrown over for a big garden party! Everything is temporary. Everything grows and comes up quickly, but it disappears quickly too. It is a lot of maintenance but the man-made and the natural can be combined."

I asked, given the huge increase in tourism and building, where the future of the Balinese garden lay.

"It is a very dynamic culture. They are easily bored. They will resist the trend for minimal gardens, because they are gardeners. Nature will break back again."

THE BLACK EARTH

THE AMAZON RAINFOREST, BRAZIL

When I visited the *terra preta* or Black Earth of the Amazon rainforest in 2006 it was a scarcely known concept, yet it has leapt into environmental prominence since then as a means of dramatically cutting carbon emissions. It is extraordinary that the local Indian population were able to cultivate the rainforest sustainably for thousands of years using the Black Earth technique. When the rainforest is cleared for Western agriculture the big timber is removed and the remainder is set alight – the traditional 'slash and burn' process. For the first year or two the ash provides extra nutrients and crops grow well, but the soil is quickly exhausted and typically abandoned after about three years. It then takes some 50 years to be able to produce more crops and about 200 for the forest to regrow.

A tiny proportion of the rainforest (however it amounts to perhaps 20,000 square miles) has a deep, rich soil that is man-made. I visited one site that was surrounded on three sides by thick forest but was rich with papayas, bananas, mangoes and oranges together with crops. The dig was on the site of a smallholding that had been continuously cultivated by the same family for generations.

In conventional clearance the fires are lit indiscriminately and always in the dry season. They rage at furious heats, reducing the material to grey ash, which in turn provides an immediate supply of nutrients for the subsequent crop.

In the *terra preta* the site is chosen carefully, trying to include as many palms as possible, which burn slowly and at a low heat. The firing is always done in the rainy season, again encouraging a relatively low, smouldering heat. This means that carbon and charcoal is produced rather than ash and this acts as a sponge for nutrients, locking them into the soil over a long period. Because it is the rainy season the available nutrients are washed gradually into the soil – and held by the charcoal – rather than being washed away into the river as ash.

After the first crop the villagers pile all their organic human, animal and vegetable waste onto the surface of the soil as a mulch, where it decomposes very fast. Another crop is taken and when this is cleared the ground is left fallow for one or two years. The resulting very vigorous vegetation is cut and left as a mulch to rot down and another crop is taken of it.

This cycle can be repeated endlessly with the carbon from the initial fire holding nutrients in the soil that plants can absorb at a much slower rate than the rainforest and thin Amazonian soil gradually becoming deeper, richer and blacker and ever more able to sustain life, rather than the disastrous contribution to the destruction of the planet that slash-and-burn continues to make.

Kirstenbosch National Botanical Garden
Royal Botanic Gardens
The Ethnobotanical Garden
The Botanic Garden
Huntington Botanical Garden
The Sítio

BOTANICAL

Botanical gardens fill a very particular horticultural niche. By definition they are a collection of plants gathered for their botanical, ecological and geographical interest as much as for their aesthetic values. This is often a kind of liberation, freeing them of the tyranny of taste. It does not, of course, mean that many are not very beautiful gardens – they would be so regardless of the interest of the plants that they contain. They are also places of study and refuge where many endangered species can be nurtured and protected that would otherwise be lost to the predations of modern man. Botanic gardens are like reference libraries. You dip in and out of them, look things up, trying to make connections, put things in context. Seeing plants in their natural habitat is always deeply informative, even if you have grown them for years, and provides an emotional and cultural context as well as a botanical one.

KIRSTENBOSCH NATIONAL BOTANIC GARDEN
CAPE TOWN, WESTERN CAPE, SOUTH AFRICA

Kirstenbosch is not just the most famous garden in South Africa. It is also acknowledged as one of the world's great botanical gardens, visited by over 600,000 people a year. It sits in one of the most dramatic locations on earth, on the slopes of Table Mountain and overlooking the south Atlantic ocean. The gardens themselves are vast, covering almost 100 acres of carefully tended land, but actually only make up a small proportion of a 1,300-acre estate that runs right to the top of Table Mountain. Apart from its size and astonishingly beautiful location, what makes Kirstenbosch exceptional is that it is devoted entirely to indigenous plants of South Africa. This currently runs to 7,000 species, although they are discovering new ones all the time.

Table Mountain is bunched behind the garden like the wings of a mantling hawk, a vast fort on the skyline. The eye is irresistibly drawn to it and the garden moves easily up its slopes, the brilliance of carefully cultivated flowers seamlessly becoming natural *fynbos*.

Cape Town can be hot but has high rainfall. Even when it is dry Table Mountain gathers clouds. Rain falls on the mountain – and the moisture then filters down the slopes to make the area occupied by the garden exceptionally fertile.

In 1913 the Dell was the first bit of the garden to be planted, when the first director, Professor Pearson, planted his collection of over 400 cycads. These plants, with their thick leathery foliage – which have not changed at all since they evolved to resist dinosaurs 50 million years ago – create a lush world as different from the *fynbos* as can be imagined.

Overleaf: The king protea is the national flower of South Africa and has a huge artichoke-like pink and grey head. There are over 350 different types of protea in South Africa and all have upright, quite stiff flower heads, mostly in oranges and reds, evolved to attract and support the weight of pollinating birds.

ROYAL BOTANIC GARDENS
SYDNEY, NEW SOUTH WALES, AUSTRALIA

Sydeny's Royal Botanic Gardens are set in one of the most spectacularly beautiful urban positions in the world. Right in the middle of Australia's best-known city, on one side they run down to the waters of Sydney harbour – surely the most beautiful entrance to any city – with the opera house facing one of their main entrances; on the other side they are fringed with dramatic skyscrapers. This is no secluded botanical reserve. It is used, gratefully and enthusiastically, by Sydney's citizens. In the middle of the day the joggers pound its circuit and at any time circles of school children, mothers or businessmen can be found sitting under the shade of its enormous and especially lovely trees. It has always been at the heart of Sydney's life and the regal appendage to the name hints at its history and totemic status in colonial Australia.

A large flock of fruit bats hangs from the top branches of a selected half-a-dozen trees squabbling and vibrating in the midday heat. They seem strangely incongruous against such an urban backdrop. In fact they cause great damage in the garden, stripping the branches of foliage as they land, swooping in and hooking onto a branch exactly like a jet arriving on an aircraft carrier. At dusk they head off for their dinner, flying miles along the coast for the fruit of the season.

Although fully stocked with a wide range of plants ranging from the tropical to the temperate, The twenty-first-century garden that is now a series of graceful lawns dominated by vast trees has gradually evolved from the initial scrub that the settlers hacked into in order to survive.

The Botanic Gardens were officially founded in June 1816, making this the oldest scientific institution in Australia as well as the site of the ground first cultivated by the settlers in January 1788. As such it remains a deeply symbolic emblem for modern Australia.

The settlers moved up the coast to this spot because as well as a protected harbour it also had a good water supply – which still runs into a pond at the centre of the garden.

The dominant tree was the Port Jackson fig, *Ficus rubiginosa*, with its trailing roots festooning the branches.

The white lorikeets are a pretty but noisy presence in the garden. They are extraordinary birds, sidling up to the visitor with a waddle like a librarian setting off for lunch.

THE ETHNOBOTANICAL GARDEN

OAXACA, MEXICO

This is a brand new botanic garden, begun in 1997, dedicated to the plants of the Oaxaca region in southern Mexico. It was designed by a local artist, Luis Zarate, and created by local people who resisted government and property devlopers to finance and create it. That sense of community is evident in the plant selection, showing plants as part of the region's culture and 2,000 year history.

The garden is self-consciously modern and not remotely soft or – at first – very accessible. It has nothing in common, in design or plant material, with anything from a northern, temperate zone.

It is loosely divided into different areas housing different types of plant, and there is no set route through it. Indeed some of the paths reach dead ends and others zigzag back on themselves. Cacti dominate, with a large square area mulched with limestone (overleaf) and a central pair of enclosures hedged by tall cacti like organ pipes transcending mere skilful planting and becoming land art. In fact the whole garden unself-consciously combines art and serious botany. It is hard to know where one ends and the other begins with narrow rills about ten inches wide running the entire width of the site, ochre-coloured stones whose edge stops inches from identical russet-coloured ones, tiny agaves planted throughout them both save in the empty channel between the two colours as well as carved wood and stone placed all over the garden. It is an extraordinary harmony created from a clear identity and sense of purpose devoted to this specific region.

If you travel around the region at all you realise that the essence of the Oaxacan landscape, art and culture is all there in the garden. This could not possibly have been created by an outsider. How many public gardens can that be said of?

The construction of the garden was a huge undertaking. The land was previously the site of a Dominican convent, with a monastic garden on the site from 1608 to 1857, but was then used as a barracks and the original garden destroyed along with the convent. It remained the property of the army until 1994. A plan was drawn up to build a hotel and car park on the six-acre site, but a popular petition resisted that and the decision was made to restore the convent. Work began on the botanic garden in 1997. The army had left it full of rusting equipment and rubble, but the transformation was made with complete popular support as an expression of local identity. All the trees were brought in as mature specimens from the surrounding hills and many of the plants in the garden – especially the larger and more gnarled cacti, were rescued locally from being bulldozed.

It is a staggeringly beautiful garden and that beauty is aided by the backdrop of the convent buildings, all of which have been skilfully included into the design.

THE BOTANIC GARDEN

TROMSØ, NORWAY

The Botanic Garden in Tromsø is the most northerly in the world and specialises in alpine plants from all over the planet. Despite being a few hundred miles inside the arctic circle, the Gulf Stream makes for relatively mild winters and cool summers. However, Tromsø has almost complete darkness in winter and constant daylight in midsummer – which is when I made my visit. There is no need to fix a time to visit the Botanic Garden as it is open 24 hours a day, every day. There are no walls, fences or gates. This openness translates into a spirit of complete generosity inside the garden. It feels as public as the midnight sun, and as accessible.

The intensity of the northern light is matched by the vividness of colour in this garden. The place positively sings with colour, with a freshness that the constant sunlight does not diminish. The mild winters and cool summers make it much easier to cultivate arctic and alpine plants outdoors than in most other botanic gardens. This is particularly true of plants originating from moist areas, such as the monsoon-influenced parts of the Himalayas and neighbouring mountains of China, as well as local plants from the Arctic.

I had expected an alpine garden to be full of delicate, tiny and jewel-like plants (which there most certainly are, by the thousand) but I had not been prepared for an extraordinary bounty of flowers so profuse that it turned a rock garden into a flowering meadow – albeit without grass. despite the effect of the Gulf Stream, growing conditions at this latitude are so restricted and harsh, with snow blanketing the ground from October to May, that their summer display distills into weeks what more easy climates stretch over months. The 24-hour light compensates for this and gives the plants twice as much sun in every day. The result is a fresh brightness decked with colour that is unique.

The birch wood is amongst the loveliest things I have ever seen, bathed in light with an incredible green lushness. The soil is very acidic, poor and damp and the trees grow slowly and thin, so do not shade out the flowers, which are so profuse that it is like a meadow in a wood. Every inch of the woodland floor is covered in flowers and grasses, all shining in the light. The garden also has a glorious glade of the Himalayan poppy, Meconopsis (bottom right), the bluest of all blue flowers.

HUNTINGTON BOTANICAL GARDEN

SAN MARINO, CALIFORNIA, USA

Henry Huntington founded the Pacific Electric Railway that opened out California. He was an avid and competitive collector and he used his vast wealth to finance collections of manuscripts, paintings, plants and rare books that are today housed at the Huntington Library on the estate he created at San Marino, just outside Pasadena and some 30 miles inland from the coast. Huntington's botanic garden, on the same estate, covers 127 acres, but I was visiting a small section of it, the Desert Garden. Even this extends to ten acres and it is one of the largest collections of cacti and succulents in the world – with over 5,000 different species of xerophytes.

Walking through the garden is like snorkelling through a reef. It is ten acres of endless green, blue and grey sculptural shapes, most of which are unfamiliar to anyone living in a temperate climate. There are flowers too, growing straight out of cacti as though pinned to them. Most of them bloom at night but the dull, overcast morning was keeping plants like the *Cereus dayamii* blooming well into daytime. A sign told me that this particular one was over a hundred years old. Cacti live a long life and the same green remains for over 50 years, carrying the reminder of every cut and knock to the end of their days, so they end up gnarled, scarred and weathered like blasted oaks – yet flowering like water lilies.

Cacti are not like other plants to look after. Drought is no problem, although too much winter rainfall can cause trouble, but the soil on the site was chosen for its poverty and ability to drain very fast. Frost is the garden's biggest problem as it may be two years before they know how serious the damage is and many of the plants are sensitive to the slightest frost.

The Cactus Garden is still not finished but a large part of it was formed in the first fifteen years after the botanical garden was begun in 1907.

The first curator, William Hertrich, had a piece of land that was an earthquake fault, with exposed, terrible soil – cobble and granite mixed together – that was unsuitable for any kind of conventional garden. So Hertrich suggested growing cacti as a way of using the ground. Huntingdon was initially reluctant – he thought of cacti as a spiky problem to be dealt with when making the railways – but then when people started saying what a wonderful garden it was, he became interested, next it became a challenge and finally he fell in love with it. He even comissioned special trains to southern Texas and Mexico just to bring back big specimens.

THE SÍTIO

SANTO ANTÔNIO DA BICO, RIO DE JANEIRO, BRAZIL

Roberto Burle Marx is unquestionably Brazil's greatest garden designer and arguably one of the few really important garden designers in history. The Sítio, an hour's drive outside Rio de Janeiro, was his own private garden and he lived there from 1973 until his death in 1994. It is huge, spreading to more than 100 acres and now containing more than 3,500 species. In fact he never referred to it as a garden, always regarding it as a 'testing ground' to trial his plant collection. Although Marx was a prolific and obsessive designer and artist, the Sítio was never designed. He would collect plants, grow them at the Sítio to see how they behaved and grew best and then propagate from them to provide material for gardens that he was designing professionally.

Despite the vast collection of plants and the seriousness of Burle Marx's research and knowledge, the Sítio is so personalised, so quirkily idiosyncratic that it is much more like visiting the home and garden of an artist than a botanical collection.

Burle Marx's genius overspilled every medium and every occasion. He could not stop or help himself. It had an exuberance that is exactly mirrored in the Sítio with its astonishing fecundity.

It transcends skilful design and grew organically, without much premediation, but directed in every detail by the hand and eye of a great artist and designer and imbued at every turn with his idiosyncratic genius. The result to my eye is, unintentional as it may ironically be, carefree, spontaneous and beautifully designed.

His work is based upon a revelation that he had as a young man that the gardens of Brazil should be using and celebrating Brazilian plants rather than solemnly aping European gardens. This was revolutionary and he spent the rest of his life designing and making gardens with local plants as well as rescuing many from extinction by rampant development and logging.

When he returned from a plant-collecting trip he would stand in the Sítio with helpers placing plants and direct their placement like a conductor rather than draw a plan or consider the planting for a while. The garden evolved through his whims and caprices and this redeems and elevates it above a mere collection or catalogue of plants.

All the planting is in huge blocks and drifts with as many as hundreds of plants creating a uniform mass. I was told that he would often say that you have to put many plants together for people to see one and it is surprising how the eye and general aesthetic will tolerate huge ranks of identical plants without becoming tired or bored by them. The relationship between detail in the garden – the curve of a buttressed trunk or the placing of a sculpture or steps – and the massed effect of planting on a huge scale is tremendously satisfying, like hearing a full symphony orchestra with chorus compared to the whistle and drum of an average back garden. The site slopes steeply and has huge boulders and outcrops of rock as well as pools, huge trees and paths that curve and slink like the astonishing roots of yet another unknown tree snaking above the ground. It ceased to be an intellectual experience and was replaced by something much more visceral, fully formed if not informed.

Burle Marx loved chance in all its forms. So he would make gardens and even buildings around unplanned purchases, gifts or discoveries. So a wall, assembled in a Mayan or Incan style and bristling with bromeliads, is made up of stones from a bank pulled down in Rio, and a huge room was added to his house to accommodate a pair of doors given to him.

He also loved entertaining and the garden has an area laid out for entertaining on an heroic scale, which is what he apparently did every Sunday. He would hold an open house for artists, politicians, millionaires and assorted Brazilian luminaries all jostling for a place at his table whilst he supervised every detail of the food preparation. This area at the back of the house, with its huge paved spaces, the enormous glazed mural and dramatic curtain of water leads straight out into planting evoking pure, lush green native jungle – growing at a rate that is rampant compared to Europe's sedate horticultural progress. It is artifice insomuch as it is as artfully created as the party place, but the two parts of Marx's life are always in sight of each other.

HISTORICAL

No garden is an island and of the many contexts in which it must be set in order to appreciate and understand it fully, history is as important as any other. Of course the inverse is just as true: there are few better ways of understanding or properly immersing oneself in a period than through a garden. Any gardener knows just how quickly a perfect border can tangle into a weedy wasteland with just a year or two of neglect, but it is a curious fact that despite the shifting transitory nature of plants, gardens tend to hold a historical period as well as streets or houses. This is partly to do with the ease with which they can renew, repair and replace themselves but also because once established, gardens tend to stay locked into position through their layout, trees, hedges and even lawns, all of which are surprisingly durable. A garden can remain largely unchanged for hundreds of years and garden archaeology is remarkably accessible, even down to individual planting holes. On one level a garden can only exist in the present and as such is as modern and relevant as sunshine, but on another, very practical, level it connects the visitor on a direct sensory level with another age in a way that nothing else can.

STELLENBERG

CAPE TOWN, WESTERN CAPE, SOUTH AFRICA

Stellenberg was built in 1742 and is the oldest private house in South Africa. It was built by an Englishman called John White who changed his name to Jan de Witt, in a Dutch colonial style. The current garden has been tended and to some extent made by Sandy Overstone who has lived there with her family since 1973. It is a garden made with care and love and the Dutch house, German furniture and English garden measure out a colonial past with elegance, style and beauty.

Situated in the lee of Table Mountain in Cape Town, this garden claims to be the wettest place in the cape, getting 60 inches of rain a year, most of which seemed to fall on the day that I visited in mid-summer. The result is a green lushness that gives the garden a distinctly British look and feel. This is consistent with its history, which is one of colonial influences and homesickness and reflects little of Africa, its plants or its traditions. It is as though Sandy Overstone has distilled all the best taste of British gardens and applied them to the cape climate.

The old walled tennis court has been made into a garden of two halves. One set of four box-edged beds is packed with a sublime mixture of English pastel flowers – delphiniums, foxgloves, verbascums, pale pink roses, penstemons, gaura, knautia, *Verbena bonariensis* – the whole lexicon of the English mid-summer border in all its glory. The other half is also made of clipped box, but as a parterre infilled with the very blue green of santolina and lavender and paved with gravel. As a performance it is faultless but it tells you more about South Africa's past than its present or future.

Despite the Englishness of her garden – including a classical and superb White Garden (below) Sandy is increasingly using indigenous plants that are exciting and that are changing South African gardens. When she started gardening there were hardly any indigenous plants in South African nurseries, but now they are increasingly available. Sandy has a nursery where all her plants were raised. "Everything is grown outside, organically and hard. They are healthy plants."

Across the unblemished lawns there is an area with exotic, lusher planting of yellow cannas, melianthus, orange brugmansias and a green, dripping jungle of cordyline in flower, tree ferns, bamboo, the leaf straps of clivia – layers of green forms and textures.

BRENTHURST

JOHANNESBURG, GAUTENG, SOUTH AFRICA

Brenthurst, in the middle of Johannesburg, is the grandest and best known of all South Africa's gardens. It has belonged to the Oppenheimer family since the early 1920s — famous for their interests in, amongst many other things that contribute to their fabulous wealth, the De Beers mining group. Johannesburg was built on the mining boom of the late nineteenth century and Brenthurst was part of that. It was built in 1904 as a house for the manager of the Goldfield company by the architect Herbert Baker (who worked with Lutyens on New Delhi) and Sir Ernest Oppenheimer bought the estate in 1922, bringing the name Brenthurst with it. Since Sir Ernest's son Harry died in 2001 the garden and estate has been run by Strilli, the wife of Harry's son, Nicky Oppenheimer.

Brenthurst was originally a house on a hill with almost bare rock all around it. But it quickly became an Edwardian garden and thousands of trees were planted. Then in the 1950s Joan Pim was employed to make changes and she was one of the first professional South African designers to use indigenous plants. As soon as she took over Strilli turned the garden organic and began to apply her own principles of gardening, which were radically different from what was described to me as the 'petunias and pansies' former style. This is no small change. Brentwood is a 45-acre garden, employing 45 gardeners, open to the public by appointment and regarded as an icon within South Africa.

Walking through the garden the first impressions are of an imposing and traditional garden set below a large Cape Dutch house. But very quickly the details start to reveal themselves as unusual – even unlikely. Grass is trimmed to different lengths and borders are a medley of grasses and bulbs without obvious attempt to tidy where tidiness would be expected. Many banks of shrubs are left unpruned – shrubs are mostly allowed to form their own pattern of death and regrowth – and grass and flowers are allowed to spread up steps and in the cracks of paths.

Strilli's philosophy is based upon the belief that no garden, even one as historically and symbolically important as Brenthurst, can stay fixed. Constant, carefully nurtured, change is the essence of its energy and beauty.

The fusion is deliberate and in places extreme. Strilli and Nicky have made a huge Japanese garden, whose creation involved six of the Emperor's gardeners living on site for four years, that is pure in every Japanese aesthetic and yet various in many ways – such as using grass used instead of moss (all hand clipped twice a year – and there must be a good acre of it). Clearly there is tension between a garden of such radical and brave innovation and the intense control necessary to maintain a Japanese garden – let alone the rather shocking insertion of a very different culture into what is clearly and proudly a very South African garden. But Brenthurst is filled with sculptures and artwork, of which I see the Japanese garden as a huge example, and ultimately it is a private garden with private and personal logic, and that idiosyncrasy gives it huge energy.

Strilli tries to encourage as many insects as possible. "I say that it is really a reserve for insects! You used to see jacaranda and wisteria in flower all over Johannesburg but not now because there are no pollinators."

They do as little tidying as is commensurate as an open garden. This of course has created a tension with people's expectations. The large mixed 'butterfly' borders have been planted with a general colour and then allowed to establish their own plant colonies. They are only gently weeded and never mulched or staked. Over-vigorous bully plants are gently restrained or removed but on the whole the borders have a constantly shifting, evolving life rather than attaining set performances throughout the season. I found this a delightful and wholly inspiring approach.

It is as though a gentle anarchy is creeping through the garden spreading by influence rather than revolt. This gives what would otherwise be an impressive but predictable garden that essential dimension of charm.

Yet there is much control too. Grass is still cut in many places and many shrubs and hedges are clipped, creating rhythms and counter harmonies to the looseness elsewhere. It is an intriguing and sophisticated mix that creates a dynamic of balancing tensions and ideologies.

THE SUMMER PALACE

BEIJING, CHINA

The New Imperial Summer Palace was built as the summer retreat from the heat and noise of the Forbidden City. It is a vast palace, as big as a small town, and the garden runs to over 700 acres. Its history is, by Western standards, unimaginably long. An imperial palace and garden has existed on the site for more than 850 years, but the gardens that became the Summer Palace date from the Jin Dynasty (1115–1234). In the early fourteenth century Kubla Khan enlarged the lake and made canals to bring water from the western hills. In 1750 the Emperor Qian Long built the Garden of Clear Ripples and expanded the lake even further, hiring 10,000 labourers to dig it out and turn it into a peach-shape to celebrate his mother's 60th birthday.

The Forbidden City and the Summer Palace were linked by a canal so that the emperor and his family could progress in an easy and stately fashion between the two. The steeply arching bridge (opposite) marks the point where the canal enters the garden.

The Dowager Empress Cixi had the palace rebuilt in 1886 to celebrate her own 60th birthday. Cixi's palace (below) is bright green, red and blue, the tiles an imperial yellow or gold, and it has a lacquered newness that is rather disconcerting. But it is only just over a hundred years old, which brings it into a very Western scale of time. By the end of the nineteenth century the court had atrophied into a series of arcane rituals that consumed every waking hour. The energy of an earlier age was lost.

All growth is formed and trained and prepared in order that it might be perfectly natural. Willows hang over the water, the reflections as strong as the real things. Willow pattern comes alive. The day that I visited Beijing was wrapped in smog and mist, but this did nothing to diminish the mysterious beauty of the garden, which constantly faded and revealed itself through the pearly light.

By the lakeside, old men paint calligraphic poems in water on the black slate paving (top). Passers-by stop and read the poems and admire the calligraphic style. As the water dries the letters fade and the words vanish forever.

The dominating aesthetic of all Chinese gardens is based upon the Yellow Mountains (left). The mountains are revered for more than their beauty. They inspire right-mindedness and spiritual purity. Poets, painters, calligraphers and philosophers have always been drawn to them to be inspired and guided. The resulting paintings in particular went on to inspire gardens. Chinese paintings can look fantastical and symbolic, but when you visit the Yellow Mountains you realise that they never exceed or exaggerate the literal truth. The real mountains are beyond all exaggeration.

Every aspect of a Chinese garden aspires to capture this harmonious balance of nature, the Yin and Yang poised at that moment before the fall. Even on the vast scale of the Summer Palace the aesthetic pervades every branch, every stone and every new view.

DOS TALAS
BUENOS AIRES, ARGENTINA

Dos Talas is one of over 800 *estancias* in Argentina and although it is representative of the type it has particularly superb gardens. The house was built by Pedro Luro, who had a general store in the small town of Dolores. An *estancia* owner gave him the job of planting a eucalyptus forest on his land, offering a price per tree and then leaving for Europe. When he returned a few years later he found that Pedro Luro had planted so many trees that he could only pay him by handing over a portion of the estate – some 42,000 acres – which became the future Dos Talas. In 1858 Pedro Luro set up his home there in a new two-storey house. He left the house to his daughter Agustina, who in 1908 commissioned Buenos Aires' top landscape architect Charles Thay to design a 75-acre garden and park to accompany the new house that she had built.

The garden that Thay designed had a maze, rose gardens, a vast walled kitchen garden and a boating lake – and sixteen gardeners to tend it. The *estancia* is now reduced down to 35,000 acres and the garden tended only by the owner, Luis Elizalde, but it is still in the same family and still a splendid example of an *estancia*.

The skeletal elms lining the road to the house make a stark, sculptural avenue (opposite). And the park, too, is carved into great avenues, once obviously neatly hedged and clipped but now tall and meeting at the top so that they are dramatic tunnels like cathedral naves (top), dividing the woods into blocks. One of these wood-tunnels does end in the *estancia*'s own chapel.

The hospitality is warm, lavish and friendly in a completely easy fashion. A tame deer nibbled at my trousers as we lunched under the tree.

The woods are fresh with a southern, October spring, with cow parsley and the smell of new-mown grass, and the orchard is covered in blossom (above). It is a hidden, secret world surrounded by the vast, empty pampas. There is a large brick pigeon house (left) built like a folly, clearly intending for more serious meat eating. The ledges are Old Red Sandstone bought in especially from Switzerland.

The garden is halfway between a lost, abandoned world where one stumbles upon ruins and treasures and a modern take on what is sustainable and appropriate in today's world. The existence of a huge garden is in itself a kind of miracle set in the vast, vast expanse of pampas here. The garden is a kind of mastery over this fertile yet hostile space, imposing a European culture upon it. The tree planting is both lovely and absolutely necessary to protect the garden from the pampas winds and I have never visited a garden with such large, or for that matter grand, shelter belts.

But Thay was good enough a designer to include the pampas. He plotted sunset and sunrise and left openings in his plantings. Garden and pampas work together to create the *estancia*. If I needed further proof of this it came when I asked Luis what his biggest garden pest is. "Armadillos," he replied.

HADRIAN'S VILLA

TIVOLI, ROME, ITALY

Villa Adriana – Hadrian's Villa – at Tivoli, just fifteen miles outside Rome, was built between 118 AD and 138 AD as the emperor Hadrian's retreat from Rome, although in the second half of his reign he governed from there. It is called a 'villa' but in reality it is a truly vast palace. The whole site is around 300 acres, of which 100 acres have been excavated.

The Canopus is a long, rectangular lake, 400 feet long and 65 feet wide (opposite), flanked by steep wooded banks, with caryatids and statues which once formed the open front of a covered walkway and a building, the Serapeum, at the far end. It was designed to mimic the Canopus canal that led from Alexandria to Canopus in the Nile delta.

Publius Aelius Traianus Hadrianus ruled as emperor of the Roman Empire for 21 years from 117 AD to 138 AD. He was born to a noble family and spent his childhood in Spain until Trajan, the preceding emperor, took him under his wing and oversaw his military career. When Trajan died Hadrian was named his successor. Hadrian inherited the Roman Empire at the peak of its power and wealth. He himself was learned and patronised all the arts, and his villa can be seen as an expression of the high point of the Roman Empire.

The Marine or Maritime Theatre (opposite) is a round building with a moat running right round the inside of the walls that surround it. Fish swim in the green water. Columns ring round both the inside and outside of the moat. Inside the moat is a smaller building reached by crossing a bridge – which was a drawbridge in Hadrian's day. This meant that he could go in there and literally retreat from the rest of the world. So this relatively small building was a moated retreat within a building that was a private retreat within a Villa that was a retreat from Rome. Now, tawny grass grows on the ground of the circular ruin, the marble columns mostly stumps of themselves. But, ruined and set admist hundreds of acres of archeology, it is a strangely intimate place.

Hadrian's Serapeum (below) was used as a banqueting hall with further guests arranged, according to their status, along the length of the Canopus. A complicated hydraulic system drew water up into the roof and created a sheet of water that fell between the diners inside the Serapeum and the Canopus. Now of course it is largely ruined, but just enough remains to give a hint of both the power and the ingenuity of Hadrian's court as expressed in this water garden – for that is what it is – as well as the elegance and lightness of touch of it. The formality, ritual, symmetry and very controlled human organisation of space that acknowledges the spiritual world in many complex ways is all there still.

Apart from the insight into Roman imperial life at its very peak, Hadrian's Villa with its architecture, use of water and use of symbolism in buildings and statues provided a model for Renaissance gardens, which drew heavily upon ancient Rome for sources and influences.

VILLA D'ESTE
TIVOLI, ROME, ITALY

Villa d'Este is just a mile or two down the road from Hadrian's Villa, up in the town of Tivoli itself. The Villa was built in 1550 for Cardinal Ippolito d'Este, the son of Lucrezia Borgia and Alfonso d'Este and grandson of Pope Alexander VI, around an earlier Benedictine monastery.

Between 1550 and 1565 Pirro Ligorio, the papal architect, was hired to design and oversee the construction of the gardens. From the outset the Villa d'Este was designed to rival the papal palace in Rome. Ligorio's design was always intended to be overwhelmingly impressive, however rich and powerful the visitor might be. The garden was and is a combination of visceral magnificence, allegory, learning and history. Ligorio plundered the ruins of Hadrian's Villa and employed the best artists and craftsmen that money could buy. The result is eight acres of lavish magnificence.

Water is the main theme of Villa d'Este and it is everywhere in the garden – such as the Terrace of a Hundred Fountains (opposite) and the Fountain of the Organ (left). There are reckoned to be 300 sluice gates, 255 waterfalls, 250 water jets, 100 baths, 60 springs and 50 fountains in total.

Ippolito d'Este was a bishop at the age of two, an archbishop at ten and a cardinal at 30. The route to becoming pope seemed assured, but he was defeated in this ambition by Julius III, who effectively exiled d'Este by appointing him governor of Tivoli. This was supremely clever: Italian law stated that a governor could not leave his province, so d'Este could see Rome on a clear day, but could not physically go there. Instead, for the remaining twenty years of his life, he lived out his frustrated ambitions and dreams in Tivoli and expressed them in the creation of this garden – although he died in 1572 when it was still under construction.

The Tivoli fountain is set in a courtyard with the original plane trees, planted in 1575, that is curiously like a town square. It is dominated by the semi-circular fountain, from which water falls like a curtain into the large basin. Originally, visitors would have walked behind this waterfall.

The water for the garden was sourced by diverting the river and all the water displays were designed to work simultaneously without a single pump. The whole has the cumulative effect of a liquid firework display. I found myself almost audibly applauding as yet another fountain or hydrotechnics display was revealed. This is exactly what you are meant to feel. D'Este is impressing his power, erudition, lineage and wealth onto you before you even step inside the Villa itself. The irony, of course, is that the motivation behind this was the bitterness of frustrated power. If he had become pope he would certainly not have made this garden here. He might have made an excellent pope for all we know, but I am delighted that we have the garden instead.

VILLA LANTE

BAGNAIA, VITERBO, ITALY

Villa Lante is just on the edge of the town of Bagnaia, near Viterbo, about 100 miles north of Rome. The summer residence of the bishops of Viterbo was on the hillside above the town, but this was redesigned in 1566 by Cardinal de'Gambara. It is generally acknowledged as the perfect archetype of the Italian Renaissance garden. It also sets the tone for almost all that has followed in Northern European gardens right up to the present day. The mixture of balance, clear axes, a degree of integration with the surrounding countryside and habitation and yet seclusion from it, and above all a sense of the garden as part of a balanced cultural and intellectual life, is something that everyone in Europe with money or aspiration has tried to emulate since the Renaissance.

The garden looks down over the town of Bagaia with a large parterre at its base. This parterre seems typical of many that one sees – balanced and strong in concept and structure – but in fact it is amongst the first ever made, the culmination of the entire garden with the town butted up to the wall. At its centre is a large fountain in the middle of a square pool reached by four bridges. The water for this fountain has run down from the top of the garden via a series of hydrotechnics and until the last century it was taken from the town's main water supply – diverted for the garden and then returned to the people after the garden had finished using it for its elegant display.

The garden is surrounded by trees and there is a distinct sense that mysterious and wonderful things could and probably did happen here. At the top of the slope, classical loggias with wall paintings of the muses flank a grassy square grotto backed by rusticated stonework with fern-filled niches. It is empty save for hot sunlight. Then, wholly unexpected, water jets from the eaves of both flanking pavilions, filling the little court with arching spray – a watery joke to delight the cardinal's guests.

This is the theme of the garden – water is a display and a civilised entertainment that rises to magnificence as it flows down the hill. Thick green box hedges flank the steps down and in the middle is a *catena d'aqua*, an amazing cascade made from stone, raised up above the steps in a series of swirling arabesques. The water tumbles down, but in a contained and formalised way. The green box is in great slabs beside it. The air as you walk down the steps is cooled by the water. It is a lovely conceit: water held solid as part of the architecture and stone made liquid by the constant play and movement of the water.

The water flows via the head of a giant crayfish, the symbol of Cardinal de'Gambara, and you realise that the cascade is its body.

The water tumbles into a large basin (right), the Fountain of the Giants, where two huge stone figures recline, representing the two great rivers, the Tiber and the Arno. Below this is a huge stone table with a rill running down its centre. Guests would dine here with dishes of fruit and deserts kept cool as they floated in the middle of the table. It is a theatrical masterpiece, the best possible setting for a magnificent outdoor party.

There is not one house or villa but two almost identical casinos, perfectly cube buildings flanking a descent down to the bottom, large terrace. Originally there was just one of these; the second was added 30 years later.

A centre basin contains the Fontana dei Mori (below) by Giambologna: four life-sized figures holding the heraldic mountain surmounted by the star-shaped fountain jet, the Montalto coat-of-arms. The stone is blackened and the statue has long been known as the Four Moors as a consequence. So the water takes us from the bosky playfulness of the top of the garden, down through artistry, entertainment and wonder to finish in a triumphant display of supremely confident power.

HET LOO

APELDOORN, THE NETHERLANDS

William of Orange and his young wife Mary came to Het Loo in 1684 to the castle which is still used by the Dutch royal family, tucked in the woods beyond the garden walls, but thought it too small, old and unmodern. William wanted to build something that would proclaim his earthly power and, above all, compete with the recently completed French court of Louis XIV at Versailles. Although it is much smaller than Versailles the statement of intent was clear – this was a Protestant court that openly rivalled the Catholic one of Louis in magnificence if not in size.

The modern garden has been meticulously restored to be held at the year 1700, which is when it was newly completed. But William and Mary, having commissioned it, took over the British crown in 1689 and Mary never returned to Het Loo again – so she never saw it in its prime. A further section of the garden was added in 1700 but William died, in England, a year later. Het Loo was turned into a landscape park in 1807 by Louis Napoleon with the original garden buried under deep sand. In 1962 the Dutch royal family gave Het Loo to the state and restoration work began in 1970 ready for the garden's tercentenary in 1984.

Today, the garden is a faithful historical reconstruction, created with great scholarship, yet many parts of it seem disturbingly modern. This is a testament to its accuracy because, of course, what we are seeing is a recreation of a garden that was brand, spanking new in 1700.

The Queen's garden (left) was the one place where Mary could be completely private – only she and her ladies-in-waiting were allowed, whereas the rest was more or less open to the public gaze. It is the warmest and most protected part of the garden – hence the 'greens' and tender plants in pots. It is based around a frame of trained hornbeams that would protect Mary from the midday sun and from prying eyes. This part of the garden has great beauty – tinged with a poignancy in the knowledge that Mary would never have seen it in anything other than a very embryonic state, and that the hornbeams would have never have been mature enough to shade her.

The *berceaux* in the Queen's garden (left) – a *berceaux* is really a glorified pergola with hornbeams planted along a substantial wooden framework and trained to completely clad it – making architecture from plants. The idea was to provide the queen with shelter from the sun whilst she walked. In fact, the light flickers through the leaves in an entrancing way and it is not in the least gloomy.

The garden is full of fountains, gilded figures, two orbs, rills and canals and arbours to sit in. I think that Baroqueness is fantastically kitsch to the twenty-first-century eye. Never underestimate the garishness, colour and vulgarity of money at any stage in history. Het Loo is a cross between Las Vegas and ancient Rome.

The garden deliberately has no naturalism at all. Plants only grow precisely where they are told. All the shapes and forms are man-made and entirely artificial. Everything is clipped, constrained, trained and ordered with symmetry evident in every aspect. This is the natural world brought to heel. The intention was to convey the message that the man that ruled this garden was in command of unruly nature.

MONTICELLO

CHARLOTTESVILLE, VIRGINIA, USA

Monticello, a few miles outside the small town of Charlottesville in Virginia, was the home of Thomas Jefferson, the third president of the United States, the author of the Declaration of Independence and in many ways the true founding father of modern America. It is a fascinating place and gave me a real insight into the mentality that made the country through the medium of a garden.

His father settled at Monticello in the 1730s, and Thomas Jefferson began work on the house in 1770. He worked tirelessly, designing every quirky detail to suit himself: he never went upstairs, so the staircases are tiny; he had a clock in every room in an age when most of his fellow Americans could not tell the time. He combined bedroom and study so that he could literally get out of bed and work. He was endlessly, rather madly inventive, and the house was a work in progress until the day he died.

Outside, the pavilion (left) looks over the 1,000-foot vegetable garden, the orchard and a vineyard and was used by Jefferson as an escape from the bustle of everyday life.

The vegetable garden grew out of the need to grow fresh ingredients for the kitchen, and was constructed on a huge, flat terrace retained by a stone wall – built over the course of three years by seven slaves during Jefferson's presidency. The orchard, on the other hand, was inspired by Jefferson's trips to England during his time spent as minister to France.

Jefferson brought ideas from Europe to his flower gardens too, and planted floral beds much in the style of Humphry Repton. The beds were divided into ten-foot sections, each for a different species, and planted to provide year-round colour. This would have seemed more extraordinary then than it does now – turning what had been a working plantation into a place of beauty and culture.

When he returned to Monticello after completing his presidency, Jefferson planted over 330 varieties of vegetables, 38 varieties of peach, fourteen of cherry, twelve of pear, 27 of plum and 24 of grape. Most failed to thrive, and many died in the fierce Virginian climate, but the numbers tell us much about the man if not about perfect fruit culture.

Monticello today looks down over a vast, endless plain of trees, like a seascape. The sense of scale is overwhelming. At the beginning of the nineteenth century, this was the edge of the west. It is Jefferson's ceaseless, restless energy, enthusiasm and curiosity, his direct connection to the land here, that drove the expansion west and the taming of what was seen as wild, hostile country.

When I was there, in autumn 2007, Virginia was in the grip of a drought and they had not had a drop of rain for over two months. The head gardener, Peter Hatch, apologised profusely for the absence of crops on the terrace or flowers in the borders. But visiting Monticello is essentially an historical outing rather than an horticultural one, and this did not matter at all.

THE MONSOON PAVILION

DEEG GARDENS, RAJASTHAN, INDIA

Deeg was the capital of the Jat rulers in the eighteenth century before they moved to Bharatpur, about 25 miles to the south. In 1730 Maharajah Suraj Mai built a fort in the middle of Deeg, with a deep moat as protection against raiders. Across the moat he designed a garden complex inspired by the chahar bagh pattern used at the Taj Mahal and other Mogul gardens around a century earlier. But unlike those earlier gardens, which are based upon order, restraint and harmony, Deeg is like a liquid firework display: extrovert, slightly kitsch and technically ingenious.

The garden is entirely based upon the control of water. There are hundreds of fountains scattered all over, which spew out coloured water during the festive season.

The Monsoon Pavilion, the most spectacular part of the waterworks, was designed as a relief from the unbearable summer heat of Rajasthan. An arcade runs around the interior, over a canal that has fountains set down the centre. The walls of the canal are pierced with hundreds of minute jets that would arch coloured water. More water would fall in a curtain from the roof into the canal. The Maharajah and his retinue would sit inside this, surrounded by all the force and cool dampness of the monsoon at the hottest, driest time of the year.

Sadly, when I was there the pools and canals were all dry and the fountains still. Deeg was in use as a summer palace until the 1970s, but nowadays the water display is only put on twice a year and the rest of the time the coolness must come from the large trees where the fruit bats slowly fan their leathery wings.

The waterworks are all based upon a gravitational feed from a huge tank on the roof of one of the palace buildings, which holds six million gallons of water. Along the stone walls of the tank are holes, each numbered, which lead to specific fountains and jets in the garden below. Each jet is coloured separately by plugging its corresponding hole with powdered flower petals before allowing the water to flow through.

When I was there it was a day of intense, crushing heat – neither watery nor festive – and yet this did not lessen the fascination of Deeg Gardens. When the waterworks are put into play they must be something very special indeed.

ROUSHAM

OXFORDSHIRE, ENGLAND

The genius responsible for Rousham was William Kent. In 1738 he was hired by its owner, General Dormer, to vamp up the designs of the royal gardener, Charles Bridgeman, who had laid out gardens in the 1720s in the new landscaped style that was beginning to emerge as a contrast to the severely formal Dutch and French influences of the late seventeenth century. Kent was at the centre of the picturesque movement that, in the second quarter of the eighteenth century, established a revolutionary style of garden design that placed classical scenes within the English landscape. Kent clearly loved and admired the countryside as it was and did as little as possible to it – framing it here, closing an aspect there or adding a folly on the skyline to direct the view.

William Kent was no gardener. But he was, without question, a genius of the first order. He saw the garden as a medium to create a series of living stage sets and at Rousham every path through the trees culminates in a statue or building, creating a sequence of tableaux. Only the visitor is needed to make the scene come alive.

The first thing that strikes you, which will be reinforced throughout, is the absence of flowers. The overwhelming impression is of green in every shade, from the lime-yellow of new leaves on box and lime trees to the blue-green of ivy underneath the yew trees.

Out of character for this garden, the shockingly minimalist rill (opposite) snakes down the centre of a path through the curves of the landscape to feed an octagonal plunge pool.

The severely classical buildings, including the seven-arched portico Praeneste (left), are constructed entirely from vernacular materials, an important factor in the integration of the very English countryside with filtered images of ancient Rome. The local stone, a beautiful ochre limestone, is also used on the paths through the grass and woods, unifying the picture.

SISSINGHURST

KENT, ENGLAND

Sissinghurst is the English dream made flesh – a castle in the garden, fading and ruined and yet grand and habitable. A castle made into an ersatz cottage with cottage-garden planting, yet with a sophistication and labour force beyond the imagining of any cottager. Geographically, it is a Kentish place, informed by the broader Kentish countryside, approached by a long, private lane surrounded by fields. And above all it is a personal place. No ghost inhabits a garden more fully than Vita Sackville West inhabits Sissinghurst. She died in 1962 but this is still her garden. I have been visiting it for 25 years now, at all times of year, and have never found it less than lovely. Of all the gardens made in Britain in the twentieth century, this is the paradigm, fulfilling modern expectations of a breathing, tangible past. But that, as with almost everything about Sissinghurst, is just another layer of irony. In a way we all go there to mourn what might have been, or even what never was.

The whole castle is built of a beautiful peachy brick and its amalgam into the tower, farm buildings, cottages and garden walls feels completely harmonious. The harmony between the structural architecture and the garden is the greatest achievement at Sissinghurst.

The first courtyard is dominated by the tower (left), a magnificent building of a type built in the brief period between aout 1470 and 1530, when the last castles were built – primarily as status symbols rather than fortifications. From its roof, the ingenious structure of the garden can be seen. Although Sissinghurst is remembered as Vita's garden, this is the work of her husband, Harold Nicolson. In the garden, as in their life, he provided the framework within which his complex and contrary wife could be free to flourish.

Sissinghurst is a castle, but what remains of it now is splendid in a particularly unfortified, rural way. It is, in fact, a series of buildings that in Vita and Harold's day had specific functions – for eating, sleeping or working in. The garden then acted as a series of corridors and courts through which the family strolled to lunch or to the study.

After a sudden downpour, the brick paths (below right) glisten between the pleached lime trees of the famous Lime Walk.

The White Garden (centre left) is not really a white garden at all but a green garden. Green of every hue dominates it. The brick paths and walls – which always look best against grass, box or yew – are another vital element; paving would mute this monocromatic intensity. And yes, there are a lot of white flowers, beautiful ones, dashed palely against the green. The Vestal Virgin statue, half-veiled by the weeping silver pear *Pyrus salicifolia* 'Pendula', is one of only two ornaments in this garden. More are not needed.

The Yew Walk (bottom left) is probably too narrow for its length but it has a kind of genius. It is always a visceral pleasure to enter into it – a long, dark corridor made unscary by the sky. Then there is the rose garden, the yew roundel, the cottage garden, the moat walk with the azalea band, the herb garden, the nuttery, the orchard and even Delos, an area of the garden flanking the White Garden whose charms have always evaded me. Being at Sissinghurst is like reading a menu or browsing the counter in a cake shop, spoilt for choice.

6

Villandry
Thuthuka School Garden
Organipónico Vivero Alamar
Huerto Alberto Rojas
Wilson Wong's Garden
The Floating Gardens of the Amazon

EDIBLE

The first and simplest gardens were always a means of growing food. But even in the twenty-first century the distinction between a garden and a farm is at best blurred and more often entirely artificial. From the earliest medieval orchards and monastic gardens the cultivation of food became highly decorative and formalised and vegetables, fruit, herbs and flowers all shared the same space. Wherever I went in the world, the cultivation of food was often the primary motivation in domestic gardens, whether in tin cans on boats on the Amazon or on verandahs or in the highly formalised splendour of Villandry. For many it is a necessity, but for everyone it transforms the quality of and the relationship with food – and the practicality of the edible garden always gives it a particular beauty, however modest it may be.

VILLANDRY

LOIRE VALLEY, FRANCE

The château of Villandry was first built between 1532 and 1536 by Jean Le Breton, a minister of Francis I, and it was one of the last of the great string of Renaissance castles built along the River Loire. Le Breton had first been ambassador to Italy and the garden that he made at Villandry was ornate, extensive and drew on his Italian horticultural experiences. At the end of the eighteenth century the Renaissance formal gardens in their terraces were all swept away and replaced by an English-style landscape park. Then, in 1906, the château was bought by Dr Joachim Carvallo who, aided by his American heiress wife Ann Coleman, set about restoring the castle and Renaissance gardens with the added element of medieval vegetable production. Using archaeology and engravings of sixteenth-century gardens he created the Villandry that we see today, exemplifying the spirit of the Renaissance garden along with the most famous potager in the world.

The potager is made up of nine squares, each subdivided into hugely complex geometric beds marked out and edged in box and arranged around a central fountain. Wherever four squares meet there is another, larger pool and fountain, so thirteen water features in the vegetable garden alone. Standard roses and fruit trees add height but the overall effect – especially when viewed from the château's tower – is of an intricate two-dimensional puzzle.

All the vegetables are eaten of course – this is France after all – but the rhythm of colour and form built up by chard, cabbage, chicory and courgette is predominantly decorative. It is a pattern based upon complex repetition and a scale that is beyond the comprehension of most amateur gardeners – let alone the execution.

To fill the kitchen garden requires approximately 30,000 flower plants and 50,000 vegetable plants for the spring planting and 30,000 more for the summer planting. That is to say, 110,000 plants for the two plantings each year.

THUTHUKA SCHOOL GARDEN
TEMBISA TOWNSHIP, JOHANNESBURG, GAUTENG, SOUTH AFRICA

Thuthuka primary school in Tembisa township is an hour's drive outside Johannesburg. The garden was set up by 'Food & Trees For Africa' and it is run on permaculture principals, strictly organic and holistic. The master in charge, Lucas Mbembele, told me that when they came to the school in 1978 they made the football pitch and put the spoil from levelling it to one side. For a long while it just remained a hillock. Then, in 1995, he realised that the hillock could be a garden. Yes! And so it began.

The garden has three sections. The largest area (which is actually itself divided into three parts) is where the Grade 7 students, thirteen- and fourteen-year-olds, can grow crops, which seem to be mainly spinach, onions and peppers, for eating and selling. They have to buy the seeds from the school, which uses the cash to buy Christmas presents for the orphaned children (of which, in this AIDS-ravaged country, there are many) and to pay for school prizes such as dictionaries. Then there is a classroom area with hay bales for sitting on (and as material for mulching) and the shade of a large tree (opposite). Everything is home-made, recycled or mended. Despite the apparent lack of valuable objects, there is a tall fence of looped razor wire, the symbol of modern South Africa, down one side.

The narrow beds are edged with green glass beer bottles (left) from a nearby brewery and the dirt paths are meticulously swept by the children.

The section nearest the school buildings is an intense allotment with medicinal plants in narrow beds and peach, apple, avocado, lemon and mulberry trees for shade. In one sweep of the eye I jot down the plants I can see: fennel, spinach, onion, tomatoes, pepper, sage, pelargonium, wormwood, cabbage, beetroot, aloe, tagetes, nasturtium, artichoke. All are used as medicine by the pupils. It is not only very beautiful but has an immediately recognisable atmosphere. It is a retreat, an enclosed meditative space.

The herb garden is both visually and ideologically the heart of the garden. But it is also entirely practical. "We need this medicine," Lucas says. "Thirty or thirty-three per cent of the children have HIV or AIDS. And some are orphans, and many have parents who are very sick. But these medicines can help them." They also keep bees so that the honey makes the bitter medicine easier for the children to take, and grow lemons to make it taste better.

This garden is the only source of medicine that most of the children have access to. They grow and raise all the plants themselves. The vegetables grown here are an essential contribution to their households. Yet despite this underlying desperation the garden is clearly beautiful and a supremely happy place, filled with the laughter of children. Has any garden ever achieved more than this?

We stop at a small shop. There are no ceilings and everything is made of wood planked from the forest. The kitchen gleams with scoured pans on the wall. Fish, caught by a net a few yards from the house, are drying in the sun.

The owner, Sebastiana, leads us to see her garden. Out the back, growing out of rickety, rotting wooden containers half submerged in the warm olive water, is an exotic orchard of cashews, carimbola with their flanged fruits, banana, lemon, pineapple, guava and passion fruit. They are rooted in 30 sacks of soil that Sebastiana fetched, bucket by bucket, from the shore, mixed with cow manure. Twice a day she splashes water from the river onto the roots using an old aluminium cooking pot.

Any idea of a floating horticulural idyll was rather shattered by the news that Sebastiana was about to move to a seventh-storey flat in Manaus. It was the only place that her husband could find any work. I asked her what she would do about the garden. "Take it with me," she said and I had a happy image of the garden floating like a balloon from the balcony.

I went on and visited three or four more of these floating gardens, including one that specialised in roses of all things, each grown in an old cooking-oil can; and another that included a good-sized sow and her piglets and a very bad tempered parrot trying to snooze in the shade of the pigsty. Best were the wooden canoes planted with melons, oranges, onions, and peppers.

As we made the two-hour canoe trip back to the boat we retraced our steps past the villages with their floating back gardens. They are almost entirely practical, a means of adding to an otherwise very limited diet. But there is a poetry to them too which is relished by their owners just as much as our sophisticated passing eye. The need to grow things and celebrate the beauty is elemental, even on a river, slowly dwindling in the dry season in the middle of the Amazon.

COMMUNAL

Few good gardens survive a committee. As a rule no more than two people can make a garden without it losing the sense of identity that it needs to avoid becoming a bland public space. But some gardens can transcend private ownership to be used and enjoyed by a community, especially if there is a predominant guiding hand that inspires and creates it. Occasionally groups of otherwise very modest gardens gain a kind of assembled identity through custom and location. Ownership then seems less important than use and where these gardens are successful they seem to ignite a spark that can genuinely change societies for the better.

'LIL' EDEN, DONOVAN'S GARDEN
HOUT BAY, WESTERN CAPE, SOUTH AFRICA

Donovan Van Der Heyden is a fisherman and a Rastafarian with a prize-winning garden in the small township overlooking the beautiful Hout Bay, with its fishing boats, yachts and a good beach. In other words, a prime and prestigious location. Yet it is a shanty town, a collection of wooden and tin huts thrown up cheek-by-jowl on the steep slope. There is no sanitation – although electricity has been got to most and the view is blocked at almost every point by a pole and a tangle of wires. Donovan's garden exists primarily to encourage the township children to take an interest in their native flora and in growing things. To cultivate pride in themselves and their country. It is a big idea in a tiny space.

Donovan talks quietly but passionately about his work. "I think that we are becoming too Europeanised and are losing that connection that used to be there in Africa – that closeness to nature and the environment. If you look at how people are so dependent on doctors and prescription drugs as opposed to how we used to live – using indigenous plants for healing. I use predominantly indigenous plants with healing aspects in this garden."

"If you want to see anything in the future preserved or sustained then you have to start with the kids because it is the only way that you can secure that future. I am planting the seeds in young people and seeing those gardens grow and more importantly seeing the seeds inside them grow."

"It is challenging to get the kids involved with making a garden because it is one of the less interesting things to kids I would say. But when you make it fun and you show them the benefits then it works. When they can plant something today and use it tomorrow to heal a sore or to heal something then it becomes interesting."

The garden is very small but crammed with ideas as well as plants, which have all been collected locally. There are water pools and pumps. Things work. Skulls, pebbles, stone constructs are placed as artfully as in many more formal gardens. It looks healthy, expertly tended and coolly sophisticated and I am ashamed to say that I am surprised by this. I think I had expected predominantly vegetables and perhaps a few flowers in recycled containers and cans.

I asked Donovan if he thought that there was a way of taking the good from European influence and constructing a modern, South African way of doing things.

"I am sure we can if we look carefully at both worlds and how we can manage the two. You can make the best of both worlds. The kids have seen the result of improving this space. They have been an instrument in it. And they are planting in little boxes, making their own space and gardens. This is for the people and it is being done by the people."

THE PATIOS OF CÓRDOBA

CÓRDOBA, SPAIN

There is a tendency to regard great gardens as being of a certain scale and weight. The patio gardens of Córdoba in Southern Spain defy this convention with panache. As people came from the countryside to live in Córdoba, looking for work, especially from the nineteenth century, families would occupy a room or two of the large square buildings built around courtyards on three or four floors. These patios became communal gardens with a few plants, nearly always in pots, and perhaps a tree for shade and a climber to grow up the inside of the walls. Since 1932, there has been a contest each May to find the best patio garden. This has evolved into a festival that lasts over a weekend and inspires great feats of horticultural display as well as much exuberant partying. In practice, during the festival the city becomes one large communal garden with a series of compartments.

In the late twentieth century these communal buildings became rarer as Spain became more affluent and more people could afford to live in self-contained homes. But many still choose to share their patios and many of those that do not still treat the courtyard as their garden and spend an important part of their lives in that space.

The idea of the festival is for people to walk around the city visiting as many patios as possible. Some are very small and intimate; others are grand, like small, inward-looking town squares. All are decked out in floral finery – with pelargaoniums and geraniums always to the fore. Although you enter from the street by small doorways into an enclosed, almost monastic space, there is always a sense of the patios being part of street life.

People go from one to the other. The doors are always open. In one that we visited the building had been bought communally by a group of friends, each with their own families. They were laying a large table in the patio when we arrived and they shared a delicious meal with us. In a completely integrated way this seemed to be all of a piece with the garden, the patio. Pots of geraniums hung from the wall and a large jacaranda tree gave shade.

Other patios I visited at one o'clock in the morning and they were crowded with families in a way that I have not seen in any other gardens in the world.

There is no sense of corporate branding or the city marketing this – although they do. The organising hand could not have been lighter. The patios display themselves because they feel worthy of display. A shared climate, culture and history makes this possible and cohesive. And the extraordinary thing is that all the hundreds of patios do seem to make 'a' garden. Each one is private and tended by a small handful of people, and yet there is a real sense of them all collectively making something that is integral and belonging to all the people of Córdoba. They are the fruits of a community, both on an individual level and as a group.

LIZ CHRISTY GARDEN

MANHATTAN, NEW YORK, USA

This tiny garden is a strip of vegetation on the corner of Houston and Bowery. It is a hugely noisy site, fronting the street, with constant traffic – impossible to conceive as a garden that one could sit quietly in, but wonderful for people who want the connection and activity of caring for a space, plants and the soil within the middle of the world's most tumultous city. it was founded by Liz Christy in 1973, which makes it the first community garden in Manhattan. Liz, along with other guerrilla gardeners, started out by planting 'seed bombs' on vacant lots, found this particular site and in 1974 got permission for it formally to become the 'Bowery Houston Community Farm and Garden', for a rent of one dollar a month.

There is a beehive and a wildflower habitat, an arbor covered with a grapevine, a tiny grove of weeping birch trees, fruit trees, a dawn redwood, a vegetable garden, herbs and hundreds of varieties of flowering perennials. Today, it is a garden that has had 34 years to mature. It has the benefit of accumulated plants and ideas – and this is usually much more interesting than a mere display of these things put on for instant gratification, luxurious or otherwise. And it is a work in progress – as all real gardens are.

First, sixty raised beds were planted with vegetables, and then trees and herbaceous borders were added. Now there are autumn-flowering camellia, a large persimmon tree laden with flattened peach-like fruit, beds of native asters, roses, buddlei, cryptomeria, carefully shaped and pruned azaleas and box, and bits and pieces of carved stone rescued from bulldozed buildings.

This is a tiny space. There is not much to it. Half of it is very much under construction and the other half is just a piece of garden. But it works. All gardens need personal and local identity to become alive. The point of the Liz Christy Garden is that it was made without wealth or power. It was made by and is still tended by individuals. It is small, noisy, and completely, utterly delightful.

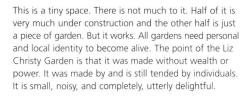

THE RAILWAY GARDEN

MUNNAR, KERALA, INDIA

The Railway Garden is in the grounds of the headquarters of the Tata Tea company at Munnar, high in the hills of Kerala. Until 1918 the building was a railway station – hence the name of the garden. It was was made in 1980 and was originally designed by a manager's wife; it now has a head gardener and five staff to tend its acre of ground. All this work is done so that the garden can look at its best in February for the annual flower show – which it has won every year. That seems to be its main function other than as an adornment to the headquarters. No one is allowed in either from the public or the employees working there. Yet there is no privacy. Every inch of it is overlooked and it exists as a constant – and eccentric – display.

This is a curious place, gaudy by European standards like a seaside bedding scheme, all immaculately kept but with the air of a garden that is passed by and admired rather than contemplated. Viewed from the road it is as bright and instantly visible as a group of women waiting for a bus in their saris or the painted lorries waiting for the lights to change on the old railway bridge above the garden.

There is lovely greenhouse that feels as though it has been there since the 1930s, but has a perspex roof and is, rather oddly, painted silver. There is more silver paint on the gate and rather municipal lamppost. I realise everything that can be painted is from the same job lot.

Hybrid tea roses are marshalled in dead-straight ranks in exact squares of soil cut into the mown grass. This aesthetic precision sits oddly with the wonkiness in all the functioning aspects of the garden. There is immaculate hand maintenance – weeds are wholly absent, the grass beautifully knapped and not a single gap in the planting – but no real evidence of ownership. No single hand.

Sweet williams, fuchsias, red salvias, astrolmerias, white alyssum, blue hydrangeas, carnations and cuphea are all used as bedding. Agapanthus, hydrangea, alstromeria, achillea are all lined out in a comfy, bulky row like elderly women sitting in deckchairs facing the sea, all dressed up for a proper day out.

The orange crucifix orchid (below), is an intense, fiery, sari tangerine and deliberately mimics the almost identically coloured lantana to get butterflies to pollinate it without having to give any nectar back to the butterfly for its fertilising pains.

This is one of the strangest gardens I have visited, locked in a post-colonial idea of what a colonial garden might be, conceived by people who were not alive in the colonial era and who have never visited Britain. In other words it is the manifestation of a kind of folk memory. It is tended by more gardeners per square foot than almost any other, yet without any function other than to win the local flower show once a year and to be admired from afar by the local people. It is lovely, charming and very odd.

THE KLONGS

BANGKOK, THAILAND

A *klong* is the name given to any of the waterways that vein through Bangkok, some of which are tributaries of the main Chai Phyra river and others, canals made to link these natural waters. The key feature of the *klongs* is that they are the street and frontage of the buildings. The gardens are designed to be seen and admired from the water rather than from the buildings that they are attached to, and yet each one is personal and unselfconscious. The net effect is of a shared waterfront garden – and one of great charm and vitality.

Turning into the *klongs* you pass a succession of houses whose verandahs, hanging over the water, are filled with plants in pots. The colour of the flowers mingles with that of the brightly coloured washing on the lines. Flags and furniture juggle for available space. Some of the buildings are hardly more than shanties, others are more modern flats and houses. Everything of course has to be in a container of some kind and quite large trees grow out of quite small pots. Mangoes are considered good luck, whereas papayas are considered bad luck and are not grown here. Most of the plants are for some direct culinary or medicinal purpose – although the money plant, whose leaves are tipped with gold, also features prominently.

The Thai people love work and money more than gardens but where the two can be combined, even symbolically, they relish them. They love growing plants that have fragrance, flavour, symbolism, and plants that are part of a ritual. They are immensely practical people, and rarely garden for the aesthetics of it – the aesthetic pleasure is there, but bound up with the practical use of each plant. Buddhism dictates that every plant has some use. Trees provide shade, fruit nourishes, flowers are offerings, fragrance cleanses, and even pure abstract beauty improves the soul.

All the plants are grown in soil collected from the land and watered every day. They barely change around the year although there are few flowers in the rainy season. But everything grows very fast here and changes from day to day.

The plants are well cared for and look marvellous, but there is no culture at all of what we would recognise as gardening. The gardens serve a purpose, part of which is to make the people feel happier and purer. But the concept of creating an outdoor space to delight in is not there. Interestingly, Bangkok has less open public space per capita than any other city in the world. There must be an element of choice in that. The truth is that Thais prefer to eat rather than garden and most of the gardens they have serve that end.

It is significant that there is only one orchid that flowers wild in the so-called rainforest in Singapore, the vanilla orchid, *Vanilla grifithii*, which flowers for just one day in March and April. The botanic gardens on the other hand are full of orchids. Thousands of them, all in pots and sunk into beds to make them appear 'natural' and with names like 'Margaret Thatcher' and, obviously, 'Princess Diana'. This is a case of orchids as operatic bedding. But the truth is that mass, conspicuous consumption does orchids no favours. Seeing a large bed of them is like eating nine puddings in a row. Orchids look best hanging solitary from their host branch or trunk. As we leave there is one exquisite epiphytic orchid growing from a tree. Alone against the sky, it is exquisite.

THE GARDEN CITY

SINGAPORE

Singapore is a strange place. We were there because it proclaims itself to be the archetypal Garden City or the City in a Garden. The capitals are significant. It is a brand we are considering, instigated in 1967 by the prime minister Lee Kuan Yew. It is clean, comfortable, law-abiding and a paradigm of the modern, aspirational urban life. But from the moment that we arrived at the station I disliked almost everything about it. Gardens simply cannot ever be good and corporate. They must have soul and passion and quirkiness and above all, individual humanity riven through them.

Bishan Park is held up as a fine example of Singapore's creation of open spaces for its citizens to relax in, take exercise in and be stimulated in. It is a small island, so such spaces are at a premium. They must earn their keep – so the park has to pay and hives off space to a spa, which at the same time must fit the corporate brief and be green and pleasant land, so is designed and folded about in a 'garden'.

This concept has moments and spots of aesthetic pleasure, but it is actually rather depressing and irritating. It feels like walking about a plan. You expect to see a design number etched into the grass or tree trunk. The public convenience side intrudes at every turn: street lamps, electricity boxes, tarmac spoils each potentially rewarding eyeful. In the context of Singapore it illustrates very well the way that the best intentions cannot work without humanity.

There was one lovely image in the park, worth the journey, of a short, elderly man taking his parrot for a walk on a lead. Both waddled along side by side, old friends (opposite).

A TRADITIONAL HOME COMPOUND

UBUD, BALI

Balinese people live in compounds, all with a very precise layout, and I visited a traditional one whose buildings had changed little over the previous hundred years. The compounds are completely practical places. Nothing is placed, planted or created for aesthetic effect. Yet even in this old, very simple compound all the buildings and shrines were stone and there were beautifully carved figures, gates and plinths. The Balinese traditionally regard trees as more important than buildings and until recently it would have been unthinkable to have cut one down to make space for a building. Destroying a living thing unnecessarily was bad karma.

At the back of the compound is a wooded area with tall trees and shrubs which might be considered the garden, although the whole compound is one entity. The back part is simply a different kind of use. There are coconut trees, bamboos, bananas and flowers for offerings. Everything has a distinct role, just as it does at the temple. The coconut leaf is used to make the little baskets for the offerings and banana branches are used to make funeral pyres. Bamboo is used for every kind of construction. Every compound has to have these three plants. The flowers such as frangipani are used every day for offerings. But nothing is especially planted. Nothing is trained or pruned or tended. They just grow.

We in the West seem to be locked into a very restricted view of what a garden could or should be. The Balinese daily ritual of gathering leaves and flowers for the offerings and carefully making them into beautiful little posies of pink, orange, pale blue and white flowers seemed to me as much gardening as our horticultural primping and preening.

PICTURE CREDITS

Katharine Arthy: 8-9, 44, 47, 55 (bottom), 56, 58, 59 (top; bottom left), 60 (both), 61, 100 (right), 101 (both), 102-3, 105 (top), 106 (all), 107 (both), 108, 111 (bottom right), 136, 137, 144, 145 (all), 146-7, 169, 170 (right), 171 (bottom), 175 (top right; bottom left), 177 (bottom), 208 (bottom left), 224 (right), 237 (bottom), 246 (top), 259, 260, 261 (top; centre; bottom left), 262 (both), 263, 268, 269 (top left and right; bottom left)

Monty Don: 11, 14-15, 16 (left), 17 (centre), 18 (both), 19, 20, 21 (bottom left and right), 22, 23 (all), 24, 25, 26 (both), 27, 36, 37 (both), 38-39 (both), 43, 45, 46 (all), 49 (top left and right), 50, 51 (all), 52, 53, 54, 55 (top), 57 (all), 59 (centre; bottom right), 62, 63 (both), 64, 65 (centre), 67, 68 (all), 69 (both), 72, 73 (top left; bottom left and right), 75, 76-77, 78 (both), 79, 80, 82, 83 (both), 85 (all), 88 (right), 90, 91, 92, 93 (top), 94 (bottom left), 100 (left), 104, 105 (bottom), 109, 110, 111 (top; bottom left), 112, 113 (all), 114-5, 117, 118, 119 (bottom right), 120, 121, 122, 124 (both), 125 (right), 127 (bottom), 128-9 (all), 130, 131 (top), 132, 133 (top left and right), 134, 135 (both), 139, 140, 141, 143, 148, 149 (both), 150, 152 (left), 153 (bottom left), 158 (centre; bottom right), 160, 161 (left), 163 (centre; bottom), 164, 165 (bottom left and right), 166, 167 (top), 170 (left), 171 (top), 172, 173, 174, 175 (top left), 176 (both), 177 (top), 180 (top; bottom left), 181 (top right; bottom left; bottom right), 182, 183 (all), 184 (both), 185 (top left, centre right; bottom left), 186, 187 (all), 188, 189 (both), 190 (both), 191, 192 (all), 193 (top right; bottom left), 195 (top), 196 (top left and right), 197 (top), 198, 199 (top left; bottom), 200 (left), 201 (both), 203 (top right), 205 (both), 206, 207 (both), 208 (top; bottom right), 209, 211, 212, 213 (all), 214, 215 (bottom right), 216 (right), 217 (top; centre; bottom left), 219, 220, 221 (all), 222-3, 224 (left), 225, 226 (both), 227, 228, 229 (bottom right), 231 (right), 232, 233 (both), 236, 237 (top), 238, 239 (top), 240 (all), 241, 243, 244, 245 (all), 246 (bottom left and right), 247, 252, 253 (all), 256, 257, 258 (all), 261 (bottom right), 264, 265, 266, 267, 269 (bottom right)

Almudena Garcia: 28, 29, 152 (right), 153 (top; centre; bottom right), 154-5, 229 (top; bottom left), 230, 234-5

David Henderson: 2-3, 7, 13 (top right; bottom right), 17 (top left; bottom right), 21 (top), 40 (both), 41, 42 (top; bottom), 48, 49 (bottom), 65 (top; bottom), 66, 71, 74, 81, 84, 86-87, 88 (left), 89 (both), 98, 99 (bottom left), 123, 125 (left), 126, 127 (top left and right), 131 (bottom), 133 (bottom), 151 (all), 156, 157, 158 (top; bottom left), 159, 161 (right), 162, 163 (top), 178, 179, 200 (right), 202, 203 (top left; bottom), 204 (both), 210

Patty Kraus: 30, 31, 32 (all), 33, 35 (all), 93 (bottom), 94 (top; bottom right), 95, 99 (top; bottom right), 119 (top; bottom left), 138, 165 (top), 167 (bottom), 180 (bottom right), 185 (centre left), 193 (bottom right), 194, 195 (bottom), 196 (bottom), 197 (bottom), 239 (bottom), 248, 249 (all), 250, 251 (all)

Robert Leveritt: 1, 34, 73 (top right)

Kerry Richardson: 12, 13 (top left; centre; bottom left), 16 (right), 17 (top right; bottom left), 96, 97, 181 (top left), 199 (top right), 215 (top; bottom left), 216 (left), 217 (bottom right)

Hubert J Steed: 254, 255 (all)

CAPTIONS

Page 1 Tofukuji
Pages 2-3 Mia Lehrer Garden
Pages 8-9 Brenthurst

ACKNOWLEDGMENTS

This book arose out of the television series *Around the World in 80 Gardens*, and inevitably owes much to a great many people. I was merely the tip of a very big iceberg working, at times frantically, to keep the venture afloat. At the BBC, the production team of Lyn Rae, Hilary Poole and in particular Avie Littler were fantastic in organising every tiny detail around an impossible schedule. I visited twenty-four countries in twelve separate jaunts, each one of which involved separate travel and visa arrangements and each one went without a hitch. Each trip also began and ended with a journey shared with my driver Mark Thompson. We have covered many miles, Mark and I, and you will not find a nicer man anywhere. The very best thing about the BBC is the quality of its filming teams out in the field and it is their work that is generally undervalued. It was a privilege to work with them. We all live cheek by jowl whilst filming and it is an intense experience. The fact that it was always an enjoyable one, even in adversity, is a tribute to their decency as people as much as their incredible professionalism. The directors Patty Kraus, Mark Flowers, Andy Francis and Oli Clark were unfailingly encouraging and supportive despite incredible pressures on time and energy. The researchers, Almudena Garcia, Katharine Arthy and David Henderson also took many of the pictures in this book and were key members of the travelling team. The cameramen Gerry Dawson and Keith Schofield and sound recordist Rob Leveritt are simply the best in the world and there is nobody I would rather work with. We saw and did things that will tie us together always. And we laughed an awful lot. Each trip also had its own team of fixers and drivers that became an indispensable part of the travelling circus, sharing every mile, every garden and every meal. They invariably added much to the quality of the experience at every level.

The more senior layers of the production team were unfailingly supportive. Nick Patten was vitally important in getting the project commissioned and has always been accessible and constructive. Richard Sinclair brought in energy and real enthusiasm and Gill Tierney helped unpick the trees from the wood. But the producer is the rock upon which any progamme is supported or flounders. Sarah Moors got the whole programme going then got promoted to exec and then again to motherhood. It was, as I hope it will be again, a joy to work with her. Kerry Richardson took over for all but the first two programmes and any success of the programme is mostly down to her work. She was fantastic, mothering, guiding, negotiating, making us laugh and popping up all over the world ready for a night out. A true star.

I have worked with a number of publishers but never with one that took a crazy delivery schedule with such aplomb. At Weidenfeld & Nicolson, Michael Dover, Susan Haynes, Debbie Woska, Lucie Stericker, Teresa Monachino and Caroline Hotblack literally could not have done more to support and encourage me. They were amazing.

Araminta Whitley nursed (and at times cajoled) me through this, read every word and as ever, a huge thanks to her. Also special thanks to Caroline Michel, who took over at the point when this book was created, and to my assistant Marsha Arnold who, despite not seeing me for weeks at a time, has smoothly kept the wheels turning.

There are two final and special acknowledgements to make. The first is to all the gardeners around the world who consented to have myself and a TV crew invade their gardens. I know exactly what that means and the preparatory work that it can involve. Gardens are personal and often private places and without exception we were welcomed and at times entertained with complete generosity. A heartfelt thank you to all of them.

Finally there would be neither a book nor a programme without my wife Sarah. During filming I spent more time away than at home and when I was here I was writing madly. She is a better traveller, a better gardener and a better person than me and yet stayed behind and held all together with unwavering support and love. Thank you.

Monty Don, June 2009

First published in Great Britain in 2009
by Weidenfeld & Nicolson
10 9 8 7 6 5 4 3 2 1

A CIP catalogue record for this book is available from the British Library.

ISBN: 978 0 297 85638 2

Design by Teresa Monachino
Picture research by Caroline Hotblack
Edited by Debbie Woska

Colour reproduction by DL Interactive UK
Printed and bound in Hong Kong

Weidenfeld & Nicolson
The Orion Publishing Group Ltd
Orion House
5 Upper St Martin's Lane
London WC2H 9EA

An Hachette Livre UK Company

The Orion Publishing Group's policy is to use papers that are natural, renewable and recyclable products and made from wood grown in sustainable forests. The logging and manufacturing processes are expected to conform to the environmental regulations of the country of origin.